WORKING WITH THE THAIS

WORKING WITH THE THAIS

A guide to managing in Thailand

Henry Holmes and Suchada Tangtongtavy

with Roy Tomizawa

White Lotus Press

TO
SUKANYA EMILY HOLMES
AND
DENWOOD NATHAN STACY HOLMES

White Lotus Co., Ltd.
G.P.O. Box 1141
Bangkok 10501
Thailand

Telephone: (662) 332-4915 and (662) 741-6288-9
Fax: (662) 741-6607 and (662) 741-6287
E-mail: ande@loxinfo.co.th
Website: http://thailine.com/lotus

Page design and illustrations by Manfred Winkler
Typeset by COMSET Limited, Partnership
Printed in Thailand

ISBN 974-8496-50-3 pbk White Lotus Co., Ltd., Bangkok

Contents

Acknowledgements

We first approached Roy Tomizawa to help us as an editor. An American journalist of Japanese descent, Roy brought fine literary skills and cross-cultural experience to the project, having lived and worked in both Japan and Thailand, as well as the United States. His initial brief was to help us with structure and style, but he went far beyond, conducting many of the interviews which you will see reported here, and often sifting out the significance behind the reports. Roy teaches at the Sasin Graduate Institute of Business Administration of Chulalongkorn University.

Over two dozen people, both Thai and Expat were interviewed especially for this book. They spent upwards of two hours of their time offering detailed and insightful glimpses into their organizations, and we cannot express how truly important their words and stories are to the forceful transmission of sometimes vague and difficult concepts and situations Expats face everyday in Thailand. The following list includes the many people who we interviewed, and who have helped us over the years not only in the production of this book, but in our quest to help make the adjustment of Expats to Thais, and Thais to Expats a little more smooth. At their request, the names of six interviewees have been left off the list. Their contributions to certain chapters of this book, however, are tremendous.

A number of others in the list contributed suggestions, anecdotes, original insights, downright good sense, and encouragement to carry through with this project. We are so grateful.

Amnuay Angabsee
Bryan Baldwin
Tom Beddow
Brian Birley
Bill Black
Verneita Boonlom
Wayne Bougas
Pierre Boussard
Chailai Jirapakkana

Chamnan Sucharitkul
Chainarong Indharameesup
Jan de Kam
Dhada Rungsiyakul
Ron Endley
Beverly Frankel
Dr. Richard Frankel
David Gibbons
Michael Harris

Michael Harris
Ron Hensley
Derek Von Bethmann Hollweg
George Hooker
Ed Hubenette
William Jackson
Kamthorn Kamolvarinthip
William Klausner
Masao Kobayashi
Kriengsak Surinspanont
Lanchakorn Kongsakul
Paul Logan
David Lyman
Prasit Tansuwan
Peter Roskam
Christopher Ryan
Graeme Ham
John Mumford
Orawan Panyasereeporn
Pramut Butra-pinyo

Jim Reinnoldt
Guy Scandlen
Claus Schmidt
Lois Seale
Tom Seale
Dow Seegmuller
Dr.Sethapan Chavanapat
Dr. Tasman Smith
Sompop Amatyakul
Dr. Suntaree Komin
Ajarn Supat Choomchuay
Suranan Jotikabukkana
Toum Hutasing
Vanasobhin Kasemsri
Veera Choochotthavorn
Dr. Viboonpong Poonprasit
HaroldVickery
Nicholas Vucich
Dr. Vudhichai Chamnong
Rosemary Whitcraft

Special thanks to Ajjima Prasopsant, Darin Parweewongchai, Ua-Aree Choodeejan, and Sukanya Emily Holmes, who faithfully typed the drafts. And to Denwood Holmes, who gave lots of support around the office.

In spite of all the contributions offered by the people listed above, responsibility for the conclusions offered in the book is my own. I shall be grateful for any comments, suggestions, and relevant experience which readers would like to offer.

Henry Holmes
Bangkok, February, 1995

Introduction

Here is an incident narrated to us by a friend who witnessed a cross-cultural flub.

A Japanese executive working in Thailand walked into a conference room with his five Thai assistants, ready to begin negotiations with another company. He began by introducing his staff, "This is my secretary; she is my head." Using polite hand gestures, he went on to say, "These two gentlemen are my left and right hand."

That's a nice touch, we thought as we listened to the story. He really knows how to recognize and motivate his people. Since the Japanese aren't especially known for praising, it was nice to hear about this one really using the skill effectively.

Finally, he introduced the last two members of his negotiating party, "And these two gentlemen are my feet."

Ouch.

If you are someone who is brand new to Thailand and you hear this story, you might shrug your shoulders, feeling that the authors haven't exactly scored 7.3 on the Richter Scale of Humor. In other words, "So what?" On the other hand, if you have read some of the guidebooks, you would no doubt recognize this gesture as one of the (relatively few) no-no's or taboos mentioned about the Thai culture. And indeed, it is fairly certain that this innocent effort by the foreigner would be quite disastrous for the morale of the members of his team. To get an idea of a comparable reaction within your own society, you might imagine your boss picking his nose in your presence, or your customer belching in front of you at dinner. The Thais get quite an emotional jolt if a colleague misuses those feet of his while communicating with them.

It is the veteran Expatriate who, hearing the story, might smile a bit ruefully, as he remembers some of his own early experiences where he committed gaffes like this.

It is easy and perhaps natural to believe that living and working in Thailand basically boils down to two things: doing your job and avoiding local taboos. The Thais, you might assume, will forgive a foreigner the occasional *faux pas*; after all, the Expat is not intentionally trying to offend anyone. And, except for a few minor cultural "details" or quaint differences, we're all the same, right?

I know it's a funeral, but why is everyone smiling?

Of course we're the same. We see. We hear. We enjoy. We hate. We fight. We love. We want the best for our families. We may not all speak the same language, but when it gets down to the crunch, we can all communicate and cooperate. You want to be happy? Fine, so do I. You need my help to be happy? Good; let's see what we can do. People are the same wherever you go—from Pretoria to Paris, from Baghdad to Bangkok.

Well, if we are so similar, why do foreigners complain so often about working with the Thais? And why do Thais frequently find foreigners so arrogant and exasperating? All people may see and hear and fear and enjoy, but it's very possible that we aren't seeing and hearing and fearing and enjoying in the same way as they are. I can bow, but I refuse to demean myself. I can restrain my anger, but I refuse to idly watch injustice being done. I can physically consume that food, but it is not what civilized people eat.

In the end, our fundamental goals in life must be remarkably similar. But it is in the means we use to reach these goals where the differences emerge. And it is at this level, more importantly than at the superficial level of social do's and don'ts, where the opportunities lie for us to develop understanding, respect , and the effective relationships we seek between ourselves and our Thai colleagues.

What most Thais want is for their honorable, knowledgeable, and talented guests to respect the differences which are important to them. If they see you making a sincere effort to understand who they are, what they feel and how they work, *that theirs is a culture layers deeper than a simple list of local etiquette*, the Thais will be remarkably forgiving of even quite serious blunders. And they might also turn out to be as competent and well-motivated as anybody else in the world you've ever worked with.

This book is a serious attempt to make these differences clearer to the Expatriate working with the Thais. Intended for both the newcomer and the more seasoned foreigner in Thailand, we hope it serves as a useful step in your efforts to deepen your understanding, respect, and abilities to forge lively cooperation and teamwork with your Thai colleagues. By including a large number of actual cases, stories, and personal observations by Thais and Expatriates, we hope to maintain touch with reality , as well as our sense of humor .

ONE
Anatomy of a Conflict

THE STORM IN THE CALM

You could see the veins pulsing on the neck of the Expatriate manager of the design company:

> I can send off a fax in five minutes by myself while it takes my Thai clerks twenty-five hours to get done. You say to them twenty-four hours later, "What's happened to that fax?" They shuffle through a pile of papers and pull it out and say, "Here it is." I reply, "Okay, when will it be typed up and sent out?" And they turn the other way. No answer. I say to them, "I'm standing here. Tell me when you will finish it? That's all I want to know." Absolutely no response. It's total frustration and I just walk away.

This particular company is a foreign-based interior design/architectural firm which has taken advantage of its solid international reputation and the building boom in Bangkok to grow from a tiny staff of three to a stable staff of twenty in only eighteen months.

The company was taking orders that would keep them very busy for another year and a half, and the general manager, an Australian, was thinking of adding at least another ten people to the payroll in order to keep up with the increase in sales. Although there was some turnover among the Thai designers, who work on the second floor of the firm's three-storey office, very few of the Thai clerks on the first floor have chosen to leave. On the surface, from the friendly smile of the receptionist to the openness of management toward the interviewer's questioning, this is a harmonious company. And yet, there are small problems that over time, or perhaps quite suddenly, might grow into emotional upheavals, frustration, and, eventually, more deep-seated malaise.

1

READING THE LOTUS LEAVES

Keeping deadlines is very important to this design firm. Coordinating between the client, who wants to move into their new office as soon as possible, and the builders and sub-contractors who convert the firm's blueprints into efficient, comfortable work areas, is imperative to the company's success. Thus, project schedules need to be accurate and constantly up-dated. And yet, the Expat managers could not seem to get the Thai clerks to properly use the Lotus 1-2-3 software to construct and maintain project schedules. According to the Expat designer, even after six months, they had yet to master the basics of the software.

> Six months have passed and they still can't get it right. The general manager actually spent about two hours with them, set up a spread sheet, and said, "That's it. That's all you gotta do." As soon as they got to the bottom of the first page, they said, "How do we get to the bottom of the next page?" I couldn't fathom what the complication was. We sat down just before Christmas and I told them, "Look, I can't keep coming down here and telling you what's wrong, and how to do it. Here's the money, go and take a course. Here are the brochures on the courses. Go buy books. Get in a cab now, go right to a book store, buy whatever books you like and bring them right back. Stop what you're doing and get what you need." And then they look up and say, "But why?" (The interviewer asks: "Is it that they don't understand the importance?") * They realize it's important; they just don't do it. Five weeks later, there's still not a book. ("What is the resistance?") I don't know. ("Doesn't it bother them that they don't understand it?") They just keep smiling. ("Do you think it bothers them and they're showing it in a very Thai way? Or do you think they are so numb to it, they just don't care?") Numb's a good word. It's totally frustrating.

When the Thai head clerk was asked why work on Lotus 1-2-3 was not progressing, she responded in an equally emotional manner.

> You have to ask us in a nice way, a quiet way. Don't shout. They (the Expats) are pushy, like when they want the typists to do something. They want it done neat and quickly, but sometimes the typists can't do it. The typists worry about

---

*(Statements in parentheses are questions posed by the interviewer.)

a job's completion, but it's not as easy as they say. The typists are using Word Perfect, then switch to Lotus, and then go back to Word Perfect. It takes time and it's very difficult to shift between programs and put it all together. So the boss tells them to go and buy a book, go to a school. It's difficult to learn because they don't have the time. There's too much work in hand to finish in one day. Besides the boss wants no mistakes, and sometimes makes them do it over again. The typists have to do it again just for a small mistake, but we don't want to do it because we have too much other work, given to us by the senior staff.

The Expat management is perplexed why these women, all of whom seem to speak English quite well, don't (or don't seem to) recognize strongly enough the need to get the job done on time, and to get it done well. The Thai clerks are perplexed why the Expat management can't appreciate that they are trying to cope with the new technology on top of their heavy workload. Problems of understanding exist on both sides, and ideally, both should try to meet each other half-way. But since the Expats are usually the ones who have the authority, the technical knowledge and thus, the power, it is mostly up to them to figure out why things aren't working out, and what they can do about it.

He's demanding another job "yesterday".

It'll just have to wait its turn. When pushed, following the "Middle Path" will serve us best.

3

PENETRATING THE PERCEPTION BARRIER

Imagine a young woman who lives in a village at the eastern foot of a great mountain. One day she is kidnapped and taken to a far-away village at the western foot of the same mountain. She recognizes the mountain, the language is somewhat similar to hers, and in most respects, she can live a similar type of lifestyle as she did before. However, she can't shake off the loneliness. When she wakes up early each morning, she feels pangs of nostalgia for the sunrise she always loved to watch in her old village. It takes her several months to accept in a small way how nebulous the sunrise is in her new home; but as this is beginning to happen, she finds she is noticing the beauty of the sunset that people can see on the western side of the mountain.

Let's consider some more familiar cases.

An European lady moves to Bangkok. At first she's struck (and appalled) by the trash she sees on the road near her apartment. For

quite some time she can't help looking at it as she walks along. And then one day, by accident, her eyes drift upward and she notices that there are beautiful multi-colored bougainvillea billowing over many of the walls in this neighborhood; quite spectacular. At home she has never seen anything like it. From now on, during these walks it's going to be a question of where she will decide to rest her eyes. This decision will to some extent affect her morale, vis-a-vis her stay in the country.

A Thai moves with his family to Boston, Massachusetts. When visiting an elderly American couple, he is struck (and appalled) at the apparent isolation of these old people. "Where are their grandchildren, to keep them cheerful and secure? Not even their children live with them; they must be so lonely." For some time, he can't stop thinking about this couple. But the weeks go by, and he begins to notice how easy it is to get things done here. "Shops are clean; the workers courteous and efficient. We can breathe the air. We can see concerts. And there isn't any traffic!"

There are three questions these stories pose: What does a visitor choose to see in his new environment? What does he choose to ignore? And how does he read or detect the things he does see?) Moving to a new environment, he immediately senses some "differences" in the way the local people communicate, in the way they act and think. Some of these "differences" may seem attractive, like the Thai gentleman who smiles after you've banged into his fender with your car. And other "differences" may annoy you no end, like the Thai gentleman who smiles after he has banged into your fender with his car.

Some of these so-called "cultural differences" may be difficult to rationalize at first. A foreigner new to Thailand might not know, for example, that a Thai may smile to put another person at ease, even if the other is at fault, or that a Thai at fault may smile with the hopes of gaining the other's forgiveness. If the visitor were aware of the rationale and intentions behind the behavior, then he might be better able to cope with these alien situations.

So there are the problems of perception, of noticing and focusing attention on things that are somewhat different, and seeing people's behavior only in part. But a third difficulty is the tendency, which most of us have to a degree, to believe that the differences between us are greater than they really are. When arriving in a new place, we're faced with a massive amount of new information and behavior, some of it pretty indigestible. And because of this visual and emotional overload, our mind is appealing for some way to put the information into neater packages. So when we notice a certain piece of new or "different" behavior, or behavior which we never saw in a situation like this elsewhere, the mind rushes to find a label or a "box" for that behavior. "The Americans are superficial." "The French are snobs." "The Thais pass the buck." "The Finns are cold." Once these boxes are firmly in place and closed, they can become crippling generalizations, which can last throughout the overseas assignment. And it's difficult to open them up again, to re-discover a more balanced view.

Crossing cultures is more about *differences of degree* than absolutes, *of similarities arranged in different priorities.* The newcomer, thinking about that car accident, might reflect that there have been times back home when he also wanted to make people less anxious when they'd made mistakes, or times when he, too, had hoped for forgiveness from someone he had wronged. With this in mind, then maybe the Thais aren't so different after all. Although the foreigner might expect an instant verbal apology from a Thai in the wrong, followed by an explanation of what action he'll take to rectify the situation, the Thai might express himself differently from the way the foreigner is used to. But the feelings of contrition and forgiveness, whether expressed explicitly or with a smile, are pretty much the same.

Perhaps if we stay too attached to those sunrises, we might miss some surprisingly interesting and attractive sunsets.

In a more practical context, imagine sitting at a problem-solving meeting. One of the meeting members is your direct boss. As the discussion proceeds, he offers a solution which you know is very unsuitable. You're faced with a small dilemma : Should you speak out (i.e., applying frankness, a value important to you) or show respectful discretion (another important value)? Which one would you choose – the sunrise or the sunset?

WAYS OF LOOKING AT THE PERFORMANCE GAP

Many Expatriates come from environments which encourage frankness in meetings, more than what is encouraged in Thailand. Thus, in most of your meeting situations, you would probably choose to be more direct and less respectfully discrete than Thais would. The Thai emphasis on respectful discretion, which may be shown by keeping one's mouth shut, is frequently *misunderstood* by Expats as a lack of assertiveness or a limited dedication to getting the job done.

But it might be time for a pause. When your new colleagues' performance is not going according to your standards, consider the following questions:

Are my Thai colleagues incompetent?

Are they merely inexperienced, and need training?

How do our cultural values and work priorities differ?

A QUESTION OF COMPETENCE

The Australian general manager in the design firm said he was making progress. He explained that his staff had finally attended computer courses and that they were also getting supplementary lessons from a computer specialist within the company. However, progress was still slow.

> They can do it, but sometimes it's easier for me to do it myself. The only trouble with that is, if we do it ourselves then we're always doing it and no one's learning. I can't take it on myself, otherwise I'll get nothing done. I'll just get bogged down and I'll be just an office worker – a very expensive office worker. And that's not what I'm paid to be.

Despite efforts to inform, train, and encourage with positive prodding and decent wages (the clerks are said to be receiving at least market wages), if the employee fails to improve, or improves at such a slow rate as to cause motivational problems among other employees, the employee could be considered incompetent. However, in all fairness to that employee, the predicament being faced by the Thai employee could very well be the responsibility of the people who hired him in the first place. Often, especially in a small, growing company where "all-purpose" people may seem the best choice for the moment, the job requirements are not always made clear or precise. In fact, consideration of the quality of the job candidate's foreign language ability (usually English) often skirts over the question of whether the candidate has other necessary technical skills to do the job competently. As a Thai manager in a large American manufacturing concern stated, "If you want someone who can handle Lotus 1-2-3, you should hire someone who knows how to use computers."

So what you may have here is actually a management problem, not a cultural problem.

A QUESTION OF EXPERIENCE

To make a proper adjustment to a new culture, a newcomer needs to look very carefully at his or her notions of what is "normal." Can Expats working in Thailand assume that a Thai secretary, or engineer, or accountant, or even manager, will have the same range of abilities or standards that their counterparts in most Western nations have? If the Expat defines these job titles too rigidly or ethnocentrically, he will be disappointed.

The Thai economy has grown so quickly that it has, in many sectors, outstripped its own ability to provide private business with the people who have the skills and knowledge to handle the great influx of new technology and management systems introduced by Western and other Asian organizations. In the case where the Expats have had trouble getting their staff to effectively use the Lotus 1-2-3 software, it was indeed pointed out by one of them that the Thais were baffled by even the basics of computer usage. "They're not even grasping the basic concepts," said the Expat designer. "They load up Lotus on one machine and it's on the whole network. They didn't believe that they could pick up the same information on another machine. They just had no idea. "

Explained the general manager,

I don't belittle the Thai people at all, but it's a situation that has arisen because of the immensity of the economic boom (of the late 1980s and early 1990s). You've got rice farmers, or people who were rice farmers, who have come to the city looking for work. And all of a sudden they're a carpenter or a plumber and they know next to nothing about what they're doing except that they've got a saw and a hammer. And they've come from such a poor background they don't understand the quality that's required. I mean a lot of these workers live in what we would call slum dwellings, and whilst they're happy, well-fed and healthy from the point of view of living standards in their own environment, it's worlds apart from the environment they're creating. And so they actually have no appreciation of the standard that they've achieved. They think it's just unbelievable. But they don't understand that it's only fifty percent of the level or standard that we expect. But it is so much better than anything else that they've ever seen that they can't see beyond that fifty percent.

An Expat who overlooks this gap in expectations can find himself stressed out and frustrated. A relevant perspective for the Expat is to try to recall new ideas or technologies that he or his generation had difficulty accepting and adopting in the past. (Even today, some of us have difficulty setting the timer on our VCRs.) If the Expat can reach this level of broad cultural perspective, then perhaps he can look at the situation with empathy, objectivity and balance, and then go on to set up the appropriate training for his well-motivated but inexperienced staff.

A QUESTION OF CULTURAL VALUES AND PRIORITIES

Assuming that the firm in this case study is not filled with incompetents, and that the typists are in fact well-intentioned and quite trainable, one wonders why the Expat managers cannot get their staff to perform the way they want them to.

Here is where different cultural priorities may enter the picture.

There are at least two powerful values that clash in this case. One is the value on attaining results: the need to get the job done efficiently while maintaining high standards. Westerners as well as other Asian investors in Thailand place a very high premium on this.

The other value is on maintaining and building relationships: the need to be working in an environment where people understand their roles and relationships and protect them carefully. In Thailand, where an intricate web of relationships link a wide number and variety of people in a delicate milieu of give-and-take, most Expats have some difficulty understanding the sophisticated forms of etiquette involved, let alone how to get plugged into the network itself.

The Thai clerks in the case study have said they appreciate the Expats' emphasis on results and want to do their jobs well and efficiently. But for various reasons, they have failed to reach the Expats' expectations. There must be a gap somewhere that needs to be bridged.

The Expats, for their part, appreciate the value of relationships with their Thai co-workers and subordinates and would like a warm working environment. And yet, their drive to excel, to the levels they themselves are used to, takes precedence over the need to extend the patience, encouragement, coaching and warmth that the Thais may respond to; the Expats are less accustomed to giving it.

Happy Birthday: During an interview with one of the Expats, there was a birthday party going on for one of the employees at the reception area. Through the glass wall in the meeting room, the Expat designer as well as the interviewer could watch the presenting of cards and gifts, the smiling and singing, and the cutting of a birthday cake just two meters away. As the general manager led his people in a warm rendition of the universal birthday song, the other Expat and interviewer continued to chat away in the separate room. Feeling a bit ill at ease, the interviewer asked the Australian if he would prefer to join his colleagues in the celebration. The Australian, most likely out of consideration for his guest, waved off the idea with a "No worries, mate" flick of the hand, and continued on with his train of thought. The door to the meeting room was pulled open and someone brought in two pieces of ice cream cake, momentarily breaking the isolation.

Was there a significant or symbolic decision here? Should the Australian have stood up and joined the party? The Thais probably were not put out by his absence; they would appreciate that he was attending to a guest. And yet, if the Expat had decided to join the party, even for a short while, might it have shown the Thais that he is attempting to bridge the gap, to get closer to them?

A Language Barrier? Relations between the Expats and the Thais aren't bad. But they could be better. According to the general manager,

> The situation isn't bad, but there is a separation. There always is When we get a big project, or when someone's going away, or there's a birthday, I make it a point to go and organize a dinner at the company's expense. But even when you sit down at a table, the Thais are on one end and the Expats are on the other. I try to break it up but there will always be this separation unless we can speak Thai.

Language is certainly a great barrier to bringing Thai and foreign employees closer together. But it isn't the only barrier. There also seem to be different expectations about how people should behave and interact in the office, creating the social gap that has emerged between the two sides.

Speculating on why the Expats have difficulty getting closer to the Thais, the Australian designer said,

"The Thais tend to be very sociable, while the foreigners are not necessarily loners, but more independent. The foreigners tend to be risk-takers; they've left their home country for a totally foreign environment. And now they're confronted not only with language problems but also inefficiency on a day-to-day basis. There's no big conflict but we tend to be outside the big family."

The Thai employees don't always see the difference in such a positive light. Perhaps surprisingly, some see the foreigners' behavior more in terms of arrogance. Said the Thai designer, "Sometimes they distance themselves apart from others. For example, if they want to buy something, like a pastry, they just buy it for themselves. They won't share. You know, Thai people are quite sensitive to this little thing. It tells me that they feel they are more superior, that they are separate from us."

The Thais do not expect the foreigner to be able to speak Thai. They know the foreigner will probably be here only a few years and therefore has little time to master the language. But they do expect, or rather hope that he will try to *communicate* with them by being sociable and concerned for their well-being, whether it's in English, in broken Thai or with just a smile.

Is He Angry With Me? Since maintaining friendly relations is so important to the Thais, it is rare to find one who will show anger openly in the work place. In this design company, there is an American who tends to raise his voice and express his anger and frustration more openly than anyone else in the company, certainly more than Thais are used to seeing. The way he is perceived by the Expats and the Thais differs 180 degrees. According to one of the Expats, the American is a very hard worker who stays at the office late into the night, "churning out paperwork like you wouldn't believe." The Expat went on to say that he believes "The Thais understand what stress he (the American) is under. They've gotten used to it so much they just laugh. I think they respect him."

One of the Thai designers sees it differently; she claims that the American is being very disrespectful of others. "If somebody is doing anything wrong, he'll just shout at that person. You know, it's quite scary."

The Expats don't feel there is much of a problem. Whereas Thais see the conflict in terms of relationship, the Expats emphasize the value of task accomplishment. While the Expats perceive themselves to be independent, the Thais sometimes perceive them to be arrogant. While the Expats perceive the Thais to be inefficient, the Thais find the Expats pushy. And while the Expats feel their own emotional outbursts merely demonstrate zeal for perfection, the Thais consider that behavior disrespectful and de-motivating.

All this is not to say that this particular firm is heading for destruction. Quite the opposite. However, very few people can tolerate such conditions for long periods of time. People can get fed up and quit, while Expat bosses may have to endure the trials of releasing or replacing employees. In this highly competitive, rapidly progressing Thai market, losing people with know-how and having to start all over again with new employees is a costly way to run a business.

A TWO-WAY STREET

The foreigner posted to Thailand is here because he proved himself well in his most recent assignment. He got results and he achieved them by using the approaches he knew best. And he would naturally assume that those approaches would continue to serve him equally well in Thailand. Fortunately for us, a majority of our usual management approaches will apply just fine in Thailand. But in certain important ways the Expat's "standard" approach may produce unexpected results, or results somewhat less than he hoped for. The Thai system—the social framework—is clearly not the same as what he has been used to. The values held in high esteem are not arranged in the same order as his own, and the methods people commonly use to solve problems and reach their goals differ to a significant degree from his.

Not every Expat takes the trouble to find out and appreciate how the local situation operates, how the market works, how Thai staff like to be motivated, or how people like to be treated when a mistake occurs. Gaining a grasp of these differences, and applying some of them on the job, will go a long way toward finding a common ground with Thai colleagues. For the business person, a practical sort, the goal is not so much to evaluate local ways compared to one's own, but to find ways which work best in Thailand.

The Expats working in the design firm believed—at this stage at least—that their goals were clear; that their own work values and approaches were logical, sensible, and right.

But so, it seems, did the Thais.

TWO
The Cornerstones of Thai Society – Relationships and Hierarchy

WHAT'S A THAI?

> Characterizing a national culture does not, of course, mean that every person in the nation has all the characteristics assigned to that culture. Therefore, in describing national cultures we refer to the common elements within each nation—the national norm— but we are not describing individuals.
>
> — Dr. Geert Hofstede

This is indeed a challenge—describing a nation or a culture's people in easy-to-understand terms without minimizing the complexity and diversity of its individuals. It is probably impossible to present all the aspects and intricacies of such a cultural mosaic. Not only business people but academics (Thai as well as foreign) have been struggling at it for years. There have been similar ongoing debates trying to describe the national characteristics of the French, the Americans, the Scandinavians and various others. Who are the "British", nowadays, with so many newcomers from South Asia and the West Indies?

But although the difficulties are numerous, looking for "national characteristics" can help us quite a lot, if for only one benefit: It helps us estimate norms of how people are likely to behave in certain common circumstances of particular interest to us in our work. These norms—about how our Thai hosts are expected to behave— serve, in turn, as guideposts in how we may fit in, or at least respond to the norms.

One observer who has made a particularly useful contribution to this search for national characteristics is Dr. Geert Hofstede, an

engineer and industrial psychologist. Spanning fifty-three national "business cultures" and over 100,000 participants, Hofstede found ways to show how these "business cultures" differ along several "dimensions" in attitudes and preferences. In these surveys, the Thai people were found to rank high in the dimension known as Power Distance, or "the extent to which a society accepts the fact that power in institutions and organizations is distributed un-equally." And Thais also ranked very high in the dimension known as Collectivism, which is "characterized by a tight social frame-work in which people distinguish between in-groups and out-groups." (See Box for more details.)

THE HOFSTEDE SURVEY

Two dimensions of direct relevance to us are what Hofstede terms the Collectivist-Individualist Dimension and the Power Distance Dimension. It is on these two important dimensions where Thais, in general, differ quite markedly from those of many western countries, and even from those of some other Asian countries.

The Invidualism-Collectivism Index measures the degree to which individuals are integrated into groups on the one hand, or—on the other hand—the degree to which individuals are more expected to look after themselves, and where their ties to each other are quite loose. Societies on the "collectivist" side stress strong, integrated in-groups. Plotting the countries comparatively between these two poles, Thailand ranks 41st, out of 53 cultures surveyed, indicating a strongly "collectivist" society. Strongly "individualist" cultures are France (10th), Australia (2nd), and the USA, which ranks number one in this respect.

The Power-Distance Index refers to the extent to which the less powerful members of an organization (i.e., juniors) accept and expect that power is distributed unequally. In the Hofstede survey, the Thais ranked above the middle among the countries surveyed—21st among 53 cultures. This means, among other things, that Thais of both junior and senior rank (compared to those of 32 other cultures) expect and even prefer there to be greater hierarchal gaps among levels of management. Great Britain ranked 44th in the survey; Sweden 48th; and Austria 53rd. All of these latter cultures prefer and expect a much smaller, flatter gap between ranks. And their common national communication patterns reflect the smaller gaps between ranks.

And indeed, in Thailand there are two norms which can confidently be said to exist:

— that Thais work hard to build and maintain relationships among a wide and complex network of people, and

— that Thais' interactions are more or less controlled within the context of a strong hierarchical system.

RELATIONSHIPS

BUILDING STRONG CONNECTIONS

> One of the people I play golf with runs a pharmaceutical company. I say, "You ought to make Vitamin G." He says, "What's Vitamin G"? "It's that new Vitamin that enables you to really get to know Thai people. It's called Vitamin G, for GOLF."
>
> – A long-term American resident in Thailand

> For most Westerners, having connections with senior management is important; but one's proven track record and professionalism is more vital. For Thais, being well-connected is *everything*—both internally and externally.
>
> – Thai Chairman, international advertising firm

Whether it's on the golf course, in the dining area of an exclusive sports club, at a wedding party or a funeral, one is somehow aware of a kind of slow dance as people gradually gravitate towards people to whom they feel related, indebted, or want to feel indebted. The *wais* and bows, laughter and whispers ripple as Thais make the best of their opportunities to network.

Quality of product is important. Price is very important. But most important of all, a Thai wants to know if you are his or her "kind of person." If he or she feels comfortable with you, he might be inclined to do business with you. And more importantly, he may introduce you to some of his friends.

> At the elite, high-income level of society, everyone seems to know everyone else. And because there are very few layers that separate the lower income class with the higher income class, access to power and influence can be easier with the right connections. The Expat often gets thrust into the company of these people by virtue of his status within his organization. In my case, I was able to find a good doctor for my wife's surgery and get a spacious hospital room (in a crowded public hospital) thanks to the good relationships and friendships which my Thai colleagues had with some doctors at a certain hospital.
>
> — An American university lecturer in Thailand

Sometimes the granting of favors for others is calculated. If the person you have established a relationship with scratches your back, you may be obligated to scratch his back, which makes the other feel obliged to help you again at a later stage. This cycle of favors and obligations runs Thai society and thus much time is invested in making sure one's associates are kept happy. Although this equation might seem to outsiders somewhat artificial or even opportunistic, it's usually expressed in a rather positive and graceful way. Most of the time it's really quite pleasant. It is said, with some accuracy, that Thais encourage, rather than avoid, interdependence.

There is a Thai gentleman who has published a valuable set of reference books on Thailand in English and is constantly asked by people to provide statistical information or to translate reports in his areas of expertise. If he has the time, and sometimes even if he doesn't, he helps those in need of his aid.

> Among friends and relatives I feel it is like a personal responsibility. If we can help, we should. In the future, I wouldn't expect them to reciprocate, but they will be looking for an opportunity to do so. And maybe if I need a favor from that person, even five, ten or twenty years down the road, I would probably be able to get that person's help without any problem. I believe this kind of feeling is dying, but it comes from the village culture. When you cook something, and you have extra, you share with your neighbor. The next day, or a few days later, she will do the same for you.

Relationship at the Top: For several months, an international company had been in the process of drilling oil from its wells. Along with the recovery of oil came a byproduct known as "condensate," which has value but is difficult to store because of its volume. For some weeks they had been sending letters to mid-level officials of a large potential customer informing them that the condensate was available for sale. Nothing happened.

One day the top person at the drill site decided to extend a personal invitation to the customer's M.D., requesting him to inspect the site. A pleasant tour was organized, followed by a good meal for the visitors. During these events, the two top men became quite friendly. Subsequently, the customer extended a return invitation to a function warmly hosted by the M.D. The outcome of these events was that the customer decided to buy the entire supply of condensate, worth several millions of baht.

The key to the breakthrough was this personal rapport at the highest level.

Apart from trying to create relationships, Thais also go through great pains to maintain them, by making sure they do not offend others by their actions or words. They try hard to avoid friction, confrontation and conflict.

CONFLICT AVOIDANCE

Everyone sees the Thai hotel engineer taking food off the guests' buffet table in the restaurant. The Thai restaurant manager sees it. The Thai assistant Food and Beverages manager sees it. And finally the *farang* general manager sees it. He says to the engineer, "What are you doing? Stop that!" Nobody else wants to confront this guy and stop him. If someone does, then next time he can be sure that if he wants something from Engineering, he isn't going to get it.

—An American hotel manager

In the above case, the American manager wanted the Thai engineer to understand that rules exist in order to maintain discipline and to create the impression that the hotel is catering one hundred percent to its guests. The Western way of thinking is that confrontation can be constructive if the result is the emergence of better understanding or a better process of getting a job done. Get a few goal-oriented types together in the same room and they'll bang heads and tables, and produce a comprehensive action plan ready for implementation.

If I tell the boss this guy is ripping him off, someone will tell him who told the boss. Then this guy will make life difficult for me for years after . . .

The Thai way is *not* to "bang heads"; it is of course important for the Thai to follow rules or get the job done, but they have to find some way of reaching their goals so that the relationship remains intact and cordial, and that everyone likes the plan, whether it is technically the best or not. One could say that compromise is a principle in itself, and is often instrumental in avoiding conflict.

An example of this, related by a senior Dutch engineer, took place in a large Thai manufacturing plant:

> The plant was in need of a new major energy source, and two different proposals had been put forward, each by a senior Thai. The plant needed only one energy source. What was the decision? In the end, the Thai managing director's decision was to accept both proposals. The decision was faulty from a technical point of view and costly from an economic standpoint; but obviously there were certain other priorities involved. . . .

A British executive offered a very lucid perspective:

> This is a society of compromise, which means that you very rarely get losers, very rarely get energy wasted in conflict. But you do get an awful lot of time spent trying to find the compromise. So the positive side is that everybody feels quite good about life, and quite good about themselves. But maintaining a society where everybody feels good, everybody feels they're going in the right direction, even though they are trying to attain it differently, is very difficult. If the whole society has to find a course of action that makes everyone happy, they won't be open about what would offend them.

> Because of the desire not to offend, the Thais are very, very sensitive. They read an awful lot into things. They have extremely high standards of courtesy. They have very good memories; frighteningly good memories. Everything you say is carefully analyzed for sort of hidden meanings. It's cross-referenced against all sorts of other things which you've known and forgotten or have never known. An interpretation of what you say can be wildly different from what you intend.

The Englishman went on to recite an incident in which his own failure to remember the Thai sensitivity nearly cost him an employee:

> When I first came here I was going to a meeting with a Thai colleague. I forgot something. When we arrived at the meeting, he said as we were walking to

the meeting, "You did remember to bring such-and-such?" I said, "No, damn, I forgot. Why didn't you remind me earlier? We could have gone back." Actually, he took great offense at this. Not at the time, but a few weeks later he was close to resigning because I had insulted him. He was doing me a favor by reminding me, and my reaction to his reminder was, "Why didn't you remind me earlier?" After all, reminding me at that point was useless. Quite rightly, though, it was my job to remember; it wasn't his job to remind me. But just this little throwaway line of mine was close to being a relationship breaker.

In order to avoid any feelings of conflict about the missing papers, a Thai manager would probably have said something like *mai pen rai*, or "don't worry about it", even if he was indeed worried about the papers. Thais have a way of directing a conversation away from the slings and arrows of controversy without upsetting the flow of a conversation.

A potentially sensitive or disputive conversation can be deftly diverted. Suppose a European spent an enjoyable weekend in Pattaya. He related his good experience first to another European and then to a Thai—both of whom happen *not* to like Pattaya. He might get these two contrasting responses:

European:
" Well, I think they have made a real mess out of Pattaya; it used to be so charming."

Thai:
"Oh, have you tried Somchai's Seafood Restaurant in Pattaya?"

Verbally, as seen here, Thais can be disarmingly indirect. Non-verbally, they can be even more subtle, and most confusing to outsiders who may not be able to read all the signs.

In Thailand, it has been suggested that of the many communicated messages which people exchange, a larger proportion are communicated non-verbally than is the case in most Western societies. Moreover, some of the most crucial messages may be given silently, such as certain kinds of approval, affection, discomfort, thanks, apology, disagreement, even—in certain circumstances—anger. However, just because they don't say how they feel, doesn't mean they aren't trying to express how they feel. The message often lies in the lips.

TWELVE THAI SMILES

A friend of ours who is a foreigner was recently traveling with a Thai friend in some remote areas of Southern Thailand. Soon it was pretty clear that they were both lost. The *farang*, quite concerned and frowning by this time, turned to his partner, who was grinning. "What are you smiling for?" he demanded. "Well," said the Thai, "if you *don't* smile, can you find the way out any easier?"

"The Land of Smiles."

This is a phrase coined many years ago by visitors, and later immortalized in the opening paragraphs of guidebooks for tourists. The more complicated story, which we are not told, is that Thailand is in fact a land of numerous smiles—and not all of them so happy as was often supposed by newly arriving visitors.

Indeed, the Thais boast an elaborate array of facial expressions under the general category of *yim*, or "smiling". Consider, for example, just two: The "dry" smile (*yim haeng*) and the "smile in the face of an impossible struggle" (*yim soo*). Neither of them are very cheerful to the Thais who recognize such messages for what they are. But these are only two of the more than a dozen varieties of smiles which are employed regularly by Thais in critical situations they face every day. And yet these very smiles have frequently been interpreted by outsiders as signals of cheerfulness, or in other cases, as foolishness, or even insolence. The different interpretations of smiling behavior may lead to problems, particularly if the situation in which they occur involves stress or tension. The following story illustrates this:

A European, while driving his recent model BMW sedan on a Bangkok street, pulled up behind a brand new Mercedes which was stopping at a red light. Behind the wheel of the Mercedes, as it happened, was a well-to-do Thai who had driven his new car only once or twice; he was therefore apparently not familiar with his new transmission. As the light turned green, the Thai, intending to go ahead, mistakenly shifted into reverse, backing directly into the grillwork of the vehicle of the stunned European behind him.

The Thai was quick to get out to take a look at the damage done to both cars. (So was the European!) From a distance, I could hear only a few words of the exchange between the two drivers, but I could clearly see their faces.

The Thai faced the foreigner with a certain smile.

— a Thai colleague of the authors

This particular smile is what other Thais would instantly recognize as the *yim yae* (the "let's-not-cry-over-spilt-milk I am ready to compromise" smile). But for the European, this was no time to smile. The story did not have a happy ending. . . .

Many of the smiles which Thais employ in uncomfortable or distressing situations are used, in Herbert Phillips' terms, as "social cosmetics." They are intended to relieve tension, an effort to preserve the relationship, the social harmony on which people depend upon for getting things done over the long run.

In this category of "social cosmetic" smiles, we find expressions of embarrassment, shame, remorse, tension, fear—sometimes, even, sadness. A long time resident in Asia, recognizing the Thai smiles for what they are, suggested that they sometimes do more to improve a bad situation than the "wrinkled brow" approach he was accustomed to using at home.

Smile, but how?

Thais, on the other hand, should be aware that when a work situation is serious, Expats have a different expectation of how one should behave. They feel much more reassured by a serious facial expression than by smiles. In such situations, West-

A BAKER'S DOZEN

1. *Yim thang nam taa:* The "I'm-so-happy-I'm-crying" smile.

2. *Yim thak thaai:* The polite smile for someone you barely know.

3. *Yim cheun chom:* The "I-admire-you" smile.

4. *Fuen Yim:* The stiff smile, also known as the "I-should-laugh-at-the joke-though-it's-not-funny" smile.

5. *Yim mee lessanai:* The smile which masks something wicked in your mind.

6. *Yim yaw:* The teasing, or "I-told-you-so" smile.

7. *Yim yae-yae:* The "I-know-things-look-pretty-bad-but-there's-no-point-in-crying-over-spilt-milk" smile.

8. *Yim sao:* The sad smile.

9. *Yim haeng:* The dry smile, also known as the "I-know-I-owe-you-the -money-but-I-don't-have-it" smile.

10. *Yim thak thaan:* The "I-disagree-with-you" smile, also known as the "You-can-go-ahead-and-propose-it-but-your-idea's-no-good" smile.

11. *Yim cheua-cheuan:* The "I-am-the-winner" smile, the smile given to a losing competitor.

12. *Yim soo:* The "smile-in-the-face-of-an-impossible-struggle" smile.

13. *Yim mai awk:* The "I'm-trying-to-smile-but-can't" smile.

erners feel that the expression should match the task, which the Expat would see as his "own" familiar sign of concern, regret, acceptance, or commitment.

HIERARCHY : THE VERTICAL SYSTEM

Thailand is a hierarchical society. This is the second "cornerstone" of the system. Each Thai person who is trained to be a functioning member of society learns, early in life, what rank he or she holds and how he is supposed to treat others according to that rank. The "others" in his life are reckoned as his juniors, his seniors or his peers.

In all social groups we know of, people seem to need to be able to identify their own status—i.e. their vertical position—in relation to others. This is certainly so for a Thai. Without this knowledge of who he is in relation to the others, he can't really function with confidence.

Thais measure seniority in relation to power, wealth, professional rank, age, merit and birth. Merit is the combination of one's ability, intellectual or spiritual attainment, and accomplishment in various areas of life; it includes one's earned rank and position. Deference is normally given to each of these aspects of seniority. Naturally, if a person possesses many of these qualities, he's reckoned as being very senior indeed.

As will be examined in greater detail a little later, the hierarchichal make-up of Thai society has a great influence on Thai organizational structures. Thai structures often differ significantly from the structures evident in foreign organizations, which can lead to ambiguity and confusion.

Why do Thais place so much importance on rank?

SAKDI NA

In the fifteenth century, King Borommatrailokanat, more simply known as King Trailok, put into legislation ideas that were already strongly in practice: the ranking of all citizens within the kingdom based on numbers. Originally, the ranking of the king's subjects had been based on size of land—thus the name *sakdi na*, or "field power". However, when Trailok enacted his Law of the Civil Hierarchy, he was able to classify and place every individual, irrespective of landholdings, by assigning the person a certain *sakdi na*, a number.

> Ordinary peasant freemen were given a *sakdi na* of 25, slaves were ranked 5, craftsmen employed in government service, 50, and petty officials, from 50 to 400. At the *sakdi na* rank of 400 began the bureaucratic nobility, the *khunnang*, whose members ranged from the heads of minor departments at a *na* of 400 to the highest ministers of state, who enjoyed a rank of 10,000. The upper levels of nobility ranked with the junior members of the royal family, and most princes ranked above them, up to the heir-apparent, whose rank was 100,000. In the exhaustive laws of Trailok's reign, which read like a directory of the entire society, every possible position and status is ranked and assigned a designation of *sakdi na*, thus specifying everyone's relative position.*

Sakdi na was abolished four hundred years later by the forward-thinking King Chulalongkorn, but the fundamental belief that we should all have a place in a hierarchy, and be to some extent content with it, lives on to this day.

Hmm, army general . . . obviously loaded with Karma

---

* Thailand – A Short History, by David K. Wyatt

THE THAI ABCs

The Thai Social Pyramid: At the top of the Thai society are the King and the Royal family. Down through the centuries the kings of Thailand have been held in great awe and respect by their people for the wise and benevolent manner in which they've ruled. The current King, Bhumibol Adulyadej, who ascended the throne in 1946, has been particularly popular among people of all classes. The King is recognized as the father of the Thai people and the head of the Buddhist religion (as well as protector of all religions), complete with the emotional ties inherent in such symbolism.

Next on the pyramid is a small elite group which holds two of the most important criteria for social status in Thailand: power and money. One observer described this group as composed of the "A's, B's, and C's", namely the senior levels of the Army, the Bankers (broadly, commercial people), and the Civil Servants. The senior officers of the Army, who have been most influential in Thai society at the national level for many years, are made up almost entirely of the ethnic Thai; the senior bankers are almost entirely Thais of ethnic-Chinese descent. In the civil service, which is composed mainly of ethnic Thais at junior and middle ranks, one frequently finds ethnic Chinese at the senior ranks, and particularly at the ministerial level.

The small, new, but growing middle class is made up mostly of the professional middle-level bureaucrats, white-collar workers, and commercial people. At the lowest part of the pyramid are the bulk of the Thai population: The farmers and laborers who make up some sixty to seventy percent of the population.

KNOW YOUR PLACE AND LIKE IT

Centuries ago, when the gap between the haves and the have-nots was already great, the elite class developed and disseminated ideas congruent with concepts of the status quo.

One such principle or concept is *Boon tham kam taeng*, which can be translated as "Your current status is due to your karma". You lead a rotten existence because you were a rotten person in your

---

THE CHINESE INGREDIENT

It's important here to mention the significant role of the ethnic Chinese in the Thai mosaic. Since many of our readers will be working in the business sector, it is certain that many of your colleagues will have roots going back to the many generations of immigrants into Thailand from mainland southern China. The assimilation of these Chinese into the Thai mainstream has been particularly successful, much more so than in some other countries in Southeast Asia, where either governments were less tolerant or where religious barriers exist which make full assimilation virtually impossible.

In Thailand, the Chinese found many niches in the market where their ingenuity and industrious qualities were rewarded. And as the Thai economy has prospered, most ethnic Chinese, particularly those of the third generation or so, now consider themselves very much "Thai." They speak perfect Thai, eat Thai food, and struggle to obtain an education in the best Thai universities. Due in part to this cultural immersion, they subscribe rather fully to the mainstream Thai values described later in the book. But whereas the " purely Thai" tradition tends to be strongly hierarchical, the Chinese tradition is less so. They tend to place high value (as their forefathers did) on entrepreneurship, flexibility, hard work, and respect for education and training. And quite a few of the males dream that, one day, they'll be their own boss.

---

previous life. She is rich and powerful because she was a good and virtuous person in a former life. You are who you are because of who you were. You can't control it, so put up with the hand you dealt yourself. Most social inequities and injustices can be justified away by this concept.

Another concept is *Roojak thee soong thee tam*, which roughly means, "Know who's, high and low". As your position is immutable, so are the positions above and below you. If your position, or rank, is understood in regards to the ranks of others, you should behave in the prescribed manner, whether it be deferential to those above, or benevolent to those below. In today's Thailand, most people feel that upward mobility is possible, but the imprint of earlier concepts still play a role in the people's thought processes.

According to Dr. Juree Vichit-Vadakan, an anthropologist and noted authority on Thai society, the above concepts were developed in order to:

1) strengthen the social differences inherent in a hierarchichal society, and

2) soften or ease conflict which might arise in such a stratified society.

The concepts were like moral codes for people of different status to know their duties towards each other.

This kind of thinking, although perhaps rooted in the ulterior motives of the elite so many years ago, is still subconsciously ingrained in the minds of the Thai people and acknowledged by many as a necessary psychological release valve for those of the lower ranks, who could probably challenge the society's many injustices through anger and conflict, but usually don't.

BUNKHUN

The overwhelming lower class majority may have been psychologically comforted by such precepts dealing with *karma* and rank, but they probably would not have tolerated an arrogant elite minority for too long. The majority had their code of conduct toward the minority. The minority, in turn, had their code of conduct toward the majority as well.

Perhaps the most fundamental value that has emerged out of the vertical nature of Thai society is the concept of *bunkhun*. As Dr. Suntaree Komin explains in her book, *Psychology of the Thai People*:

> *Bunkhun*, or indebted goodness, is a psychological bond between someone who, out of sheer kindness and sincerity, renders another person the needed help and favor, and the latter's remembering of the goodness done and his ever-readiness to reciprocate the kindness.

As indicated by the definition, there are two aspects involved in *bunkhun*. The first is called *katanyoo rookhun*, which can be trans-

lated into the words "gratitude and indebtedness". As Dr. Juree explains, "One must appreciate those who have done favors for one. A child should feel great gratitude and indebtedness to his or her parents, as should student to teacher, servant to master, or a friend to another friend who has helped him or her." This feeling of gratitude and indebtedness also results in action, as the receiver of the favor does his best to reciprocate the favor.

The second aspect of *bunkhun* is called *mettaa karunaa*, or the quality of being "merciful and kind". This quality is particularly applicable to interactions between people of different status levels where the superior and strong person behaves benevolently to those below him. A boss should be forgiving of a subordinate who has made a big mistake. A teacher should be generous with time and effort in order to help his students. A rich person should be generous with tips to servants and donations to beggars.

The two *bunkhun* elements are played back and forth in a long cycle that ensures a respectful relationship between two people.

31

For example, a subordinate makes a mistake that negatively affects a customer. The boss covers and protects the subordinate by taking care of the problem. The subordinate, grateful, works extra hard on another difficult project. On the successful completion of the project, the boss praises the subordinate and treats the subordinate and his co-workers to an extravagant dinner. It is possible for this *bunkhun* relationship to continue until the death of one of the parties. It may even extend into the family of the parties involved, sending the relationship on a fruitful and endless continuum.

In Thailand, the concept of *bunkhun* is played throughout and between all levels in the social hierarchy, creating a behavioral pattern by which people of different statuses can interact in a civil and friendly manner. According to Dr. Suntaree, the Thais consider *bunkhun* one of their most important values, if not the most important. "The Thai are brought up to value this process of gratefulness – the process of reciprocity of goodness done, and the ever-readiness to reciprocate. Time and distance are not the factors to diminish the *bunkhun*."

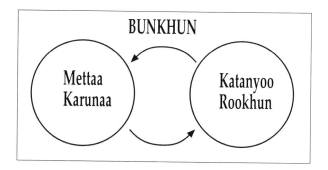

IMPLICATIONS FOR EXPATRIATE ORGANIZATIONS

In many Western nations, particularly Australia, the United States, or the Scandinavian countries, there are long traditions of egalitarianism—that all men are created equal, or at least have equal opportunities. Such a concept has been more of an ideal than an accurate description of actual social practice in those societies, but they still lay stress on equality in many aspects of everyday life. For historic and economic reasons, these countries have rather flat,

Can I influence my boss?

Of course I can. I'm the expert!

somewhat diamond-shaped social structures with a small upper class, a small lower class and an enormous middle class.

Bringing such egalitarian systems and values to socially hierarchal Thailand can create a myriad of problems, most prominently in the areas of communication, sharing of information, staff loyalty, and language – both verbal and non-verbal.

Lines of Communication:

When I came in as a young guy, I was in more of a support function so I didn't have many people under me. To get things done, I followed the normal hierarchy. "You are my number two man. You do this job. And then, you delegate." But a lot of times, it turned out there was an informal structure, one which was based on age, time spent in the company, family connections, whatever. There were people in the organization—they could have been in completely different sections—who had to be informed, who had to be nurtured to get a project through. I had to work with all levels but I couldn't actually say, "If you don't do it, you're fired." So I had to find out who to respect, who I should make sure to "run things by" and consult.

—Danish executive, shipping firm

Despite the egalitarian nature of western social structures, hierarchies do of course exist, though in most cases they are much flatter than in most Asian countries. Hierarchy, which is the backbone of governmental and private organizations, provides clear-cut ranks, channels and chains of command. Hierarchies provide guidelines which are understood to be a part of a person's working or "professional" behavior. But when a western member of the work hierarchy steps out and seeks social interaction, he or she often tries to minimize the gaps in ranking with others; he adopts a more informal or "equal" social style. Thais, on the other hand, tend to keep their occupational rank in the eyes of others, both on and off the job.

Loyalty and Turnover:

> The frustration we've found here and at other hotels is that we see the senior person leave, but that senior person won't leave on his own. He'll leave with a number of other people. Moving the loyalty away from the individual to the corporate entity is a very, very difficult process.
>
> —Australian hotel manager

In recent years, as the Thai economy has accelerated, salary and promotion factors have become more significant. Thais in their twenties and thirties, particularly those who have been educated overseas, find that their skills are in such great demand that they are willing to change jobs quite suddenly if the price is right. Managers, both Thai and Expat, bemoan the fact that they often cannot keep key personnel, nor can they instill a sense of loyalty in their recruits.

And yet, Thais can and will display strong loyalty. Unfortunately for many managing directors, this loyalty is not directed where they want it to be.

In a successful Thai work group, there can be a strong bond between boss and worker, where the boss's role in the formal organizational hierarchy is less significant than his informal role in his colleagues' social hierarchy. The senior is expected to provide direction, control, protection as well as emotional support, looking after the needs of his colleagues and staff, much like a prosperous father might do. This support is strongly *personal* in nature. In the West or Japan, such services and protection are often provided by the *institution*—a company itself or by the government. Provident funds and government social security programs take care of some of these functions.

In Thailand, as a part of this personal effort, the senior person has tended to assume a wider range of company-related roles than an Expat manager might be expected to perform at home. Among these may be attending religious events, gift-giving and receiving, entertaining staff and having quite a lot of knowledge of subordinates' family situations. In the old days, if a Thai staff member got sick, a traditional Thai manager would look after him or her. Even today, if an employee's child needs an educational loan, the boss may be willing to assist. If an employee dies, the manager may sponsor an evening prayer at the temple. All of these can serve as motivators on the part of the leader, and are commonly admired by his colleagues, while the junior reciprocates with good performance and, very important, loyalty . *Indeed, loyalty has by custom been expressed more towards an individual than towards an organization or one's profession.* As a consequence, the manager works especially hard to develop and maintain good personal relationships with his staff.

Two-way Communication:

I am a little different from other Thais because when I'm in a meeting and I have an opinion, I'm not afraid to say it. The problem is that after I leave the meeting, I would go to the toilet and a fellow Thai would say to me, "I don't think the boss's plan is any good." I tell him, "Well, why didn't you say so in the meeting?"

—Thai manager, American manufacturing firm

Due to the hierarchical nature of the society, and the "power-distance gap" mentioned earlier, communication has tended to be from the top down. Thai tradition has encouraged junior family members and young students to absorb rather than initiate, to "get it right" rather than to question or express opinions, especially dissenting ones. The result of this pattern is that most Thais—even at rather senior levels—have not had such extensive practice in expressing themselves in an assertive way, in either Thai or English.

Today, increasing numbers of young Thais entering the job market prefer an international organization to a more traditional business because they see a greater opportunity to be recognized for competence rather than seniority as in the past. Yet at the same time, they may run into problems if their Thai or foreign boss is not receptive or encouraging to new ideas, or if they themselves lack self-confidence or skills to express those ideas effectively. Many

Thais, both seniors and subordinates, believe it is the boss's job to know what is going on, not the subordinate's to volunteer information without being specifically asked by the boss. The degree to which the foreign manager can draw out and develop these assertive skills of self-expression will be a major factor in his or her effectiveness as a manager, and have a major effect on communication and morale.

Head to Foot – The Body Hierarchy:

Just as Thai social structure is arranged in ranks, so too, are the parts of the body. They have a hierarchy of their own. Accordingly, the head is the locus of the soul,*winyaan*, and is treated by others with the greatest respect. Touching the heads of adults is generally avoided. Thais often go to some length not to reach or interpose themselves over another person's head or head space.

An exception regarding touching of the head is made when it comes to children. Up until the age of about ten, children in Thailand are frequently fondled and often people run their fingers through their hair, affectionately pinch thier cheeks or even bite them playfully. After this age, however, the practice of touching someone's head seems to be found (omitting the pinching and biting) mainly among teammates celebrating a goal in football matches. In Thai boxing, the intention to kick the hell out of the opponent's head also does not follow these rules, rather the rules of fighting, in which just about anything goes, predominates. (It's an interesting reminder that social customs are not always consistent.)

By the same token, the foot is regarded as being much inferior to the foot in western societies. Thus it is usually not used as a tool to point with or to open doors. This custom would be of interest to foreign advisers in agriculture. When visiting projects in the field it might be natural, and very convenient, to want to show your admiration for a certain crop of cabbages or an irrigation ditch by "pointing" to it with a foot. Hotel managers might also point out an incorrect way of making a bed, again, with the convenient foot.

For the foreigner, who has no such "body-part" hierarchy, this would normally be an efficient way to get his point across. For the

Thai farmer or room maid, unexposed to outside ways, it is actually seen as an insult, an act of superiority.

There was a case of a factory manager whose company had recently built a new plant far across town from the old one. He was a good planner and concerned about his managers' welfare. He also wanted them to look forward to moving to this new location in spite of the longer drive from most of their homes. So, even before the tables and chairs had been moved in, he organized a tour for them to see the impressive facilities and their own new offices.

All he had was a huge blueprint which he spread out on the new factory floor. As the senior Thai managers stood around the chart, he indicated on the sheet with his foot, "Right, Somsak, you'll be here; Jiraporn, here's your office right there on the corner", and so on . . . .

Me to You – The Language Hierarchy:

For a Thai, in order to be polite in the appropriate way he must establish what his relative status is, through a number of indicators. Once he knows that, his choice of pronouns and other linguistic forms will be in keeping with that relationship. The language has its ways of reflecting rank, age differences, social distance, or intimacy of a relationship to a degree of sophistication that Westerners are unused to. In some cases, the relationship is expressed mainly through tone of voice.

A case in point is a story of a young American who came to work in Thailand under sponsorship of the Peace Corps. Rob had excellent credentials. He had a bachelor's degree from Yale, majoring in physics and Greek. He had two years' experience right after college working with an internationally-oriented manufacturing company. And then, before coming to Thailand to become a teacher, he took an intensive three-month course in the Thai language. So when he got off the plane in Bangkok, he was already pretty good at speaking Thai.

In fact, by the end of his two-year assignment, he emerged as the best Thai speaker among all the Americans in his group. He was such a "showpiece," in fact, that someone suggested arranging a brief interview, or courtesy call, between Rob and the Thai Minister of Education—who was technically his very big boss. When the interview—conducted, naturally in Thai—was over, and they were saying goodbye, the Thai Minister said to Rob, "You really do speak Thai very well indeed, Rob. The only thing is, *you don't speak it quite sweetly enough.*"

Some foreigners have observed that when they join an ongoing conversation among a group of Thais, even though the Thais all speak English fluently, they may continue to speak in Thai in spite of the visitor. To the foreigner this behavior may seem rude, but the reason may be this: When Thais are forced to speak English they are denied the much larger array of suitable pronouns which allow them to express subtle gradations, and hence adequate regard for one another. How can they convey respect to a senior Thai with the very egalitarian pronoun "You"?

As one observer expressed it, Thai language serves as the expression of "respect among non-equals."

THREE

The Three Circles of Thailand

At tourist attractions what really gets me is that I am charged 120 baht whereas the Thai only has to pay sixty. It's not as if it's a lot of money, but it's the principle of the thing.

When I go to this department store, especially in the clothing section, the sales girls are always pursuing me aggressively to buy things I don't want. I'm looking at blue shirts, they push pink ones in my face. It's nothing like the well-mannered Thai people I expected.

— Some comments from foreigners in Bangkok

SOCIAL CIRCLES

The newcomer to Thailand hears this litany so often:

Thais are so polite.
What a friendly people they are.
You always see them smiling.
You won't find a more considerate people.

Compounded by the guide books they read and the wonderful service they receive in the Thai airlines, hotels and resorts, foreigners are usually struck by the good-naturedness of the Thais. After their week of sightseeing in the cities and sunning on the beaches, many go home with a warm regard for the country and its people. Krung Thep, after all, really is a city of angels.

Stay a little longer and you begin to see all is not as it seems. Slowly, almost disbelievingly, you begin to realize that there's an inconsiderate, sometimes coarse, sometimes mean side to the Thai that stands in great contrast to the "angels" you encountered during your tourist days: the taxi driver who says he doesn't have the change, forcing you to leave a forty percent tip; the customers who disregard the queue and most impolitely squeeze in front of you at the service counter; the irresponsible citizens who throw garbage into the canals and on the beaches without a thought for others.

Is this a split-personality trait of the Thais? Your personnel manager, Malee, is such a loving, devoted mother. At the office she is courteous and kind. But should you meet her in traffic, watch out! She drives in a way you never would have imagined. How could this be the same lady?

For the answers we have to look, not into the vertical or hierarchal perspective, but into the horizontal perspective, the view from above.

THE FAMILY CIRCLE

Every individual (Thai or otherwise) may be seen to operate in roughly three different "circles". A Thai's innermost circle, of course, is his immediate family. In this Family Circle, the individual is closely intertwined with the fortunes of the other family members. There are, naturally, ranks within this "first circle" as well as guidelines about mutual rights, duties and respect; but there is also a degree of informality and a free flow of communication.

Blood is thicker than water. Compared to the West where nuclear families have become more of a desire and necessity, some say blood ties may even be thicker here in Asia. For those who can afford it, grandparents often live with their grandchildren in three-generation households. Aunts and uncles are often called on to help in those no-questions-asked family complications. Like families everywhere, your mother is more likely to forgive you for certain offenses than non-family members, or the law for that matter.

THE CAUTIOUS CIRCLE

Members of your Family Circle may forgive you your transgressions and mistakes. Members of the Cautious Circle may not be so forgiving.

41

This second circle comprises of people with whom the Thai individual interacts on a frequent but more "official" basis: his work colleagues, his doctor, his children's school teacher, his tailor, even a regular market lady. It is in this circle where behavior tends to be "proper" Thai behavior—courteous, cautious, deferential, friendly, *but* somewhat formal. The reason for the high standard of manners in the Cautious Circle is the fact that the Thai depends on these associations regularly, for day-to-day survival. And he or she expects to rely on those associations for perhaps years to come. Because of the frequency of contact, each side in these relationships has a certain continuing sanction or *leverage* on the other. Each side wants to keep the relationship functioning smoothly for the good of both. The existence of this personal, face-to-face leverage —social control, really—maintains the standard of behavior.

The elements which make up this "standard of behavior" are directly relevant to the foreigner who operates most of the time in this second circle, namely the Thai work place. The latter part of this chapter examines these elements, particularly the values and behavior which Thais expect of each other in the Cautious Circle.

The Thai Horizontal System

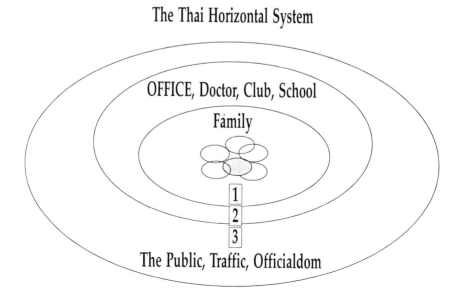

OFFICE, Doctor, Club, School

Family

1
2
3

The Public, Traffic, Officialdom

THE SELFISH CIRCLE

The third circle, or what can be called the Selfish Circle, is the outside world. As the Thai ventures outside the long-time regular contacts which he has developed in the Cautious Circle, he sees a completely different standard of behavior.

It is in the Selfish Circle where one's high standing in the community doesn't get any recognition; nobody seems to notice, or care. It is the arena where a foreigner hears Thai street boys call, "Hey you", where she is grossly overcharged, where her place at the movie queue is brusquely usurped, where the government clerk treats her coldly. Here, rather than in the other circles, we also see most of the examples of littering, spitting, loud talking, bumping into one another, or other "selfish" behavior.

The feature which these Selfish Circle situations share is that they are one-time-only contacts, in which each individual feels little ability to influence others. There is no leverage. In this third circle, each person feels a trifle anonymous, which means that nobody will recognize him as anyone special, and he cannot readily induce others to treat him courteously. Anyone who has tried, while driving in the wrong traffic lane, to get back into the correct lane, knows how helpless he is without the familiar leverage of the second circle. In the third circle, a person feels it's every man for himself, and he consequently develops a certain array of skills to cope effectively there, in that impersonal, indifferent arena.

It's safe to assume that other countries also have circles like these, where citizens learn to switch their roles and behavior as they move from one circle to another. But the relevant point for us is that Thais behave somewhat differently in their Selfish Circle than we do in ours.

What's the explanation for the abrasiveness and other problems of social behavior found in the third circle? To some extent they are caused by the immense mobility and population growth in Bangkok over recent years. The influx of migrants from up-country who know little about city life and the requirements of mass living, has caused many new problems. Migrants (and lots of long time residents too) don't always see the cumulative effects of one plastic bag, tossed out by many people. Governments of much of the industrialized world impose and enforce heavy fines for littering. In order to solve problems with bus crowds, cities like Hong Kong installed stiles for pedestrians years ago in order to channel them into orderly queues at bus stops. In Bangkok, however, although orderly queues are occasionally sighted, public laws in regards to littering are not yet well enforced. Education on these matters, whereby people could become more aware of the needs of crowded public living, has not yet become a part of the school system.

Another reason for the contrast between the behavior evident in circle two and circle three may be found in the "collectivist" nature of Thai society. The survival of a person within a collectivist society is strongly related to the allegiance one shows to his *own* group, without paying much attention to people outside it.

According to Harry C. Triandis, a psychologist and leading scholar on the differences between individualistic and collectivist societies:

If I could find your car I'd flatten all your tires!

I had to wait 10 minutes to make this call. I'm not getting off the line that quickly.

Collectivist societies put high value on self-discipline, accepting one's position in life, honoring parents and elders, and preserving one's public image for the sake of the group. While collectivists are very nice to those who are members of their own groups, they can be very nasty, competitive and uncooperative toward those who aren't. There is an unquestioned obedience in one's own group and even willingness to fight and die for it, and a distrust of those in other groups.

SOME FUNDAMENTAL THAI VALUES FOR NAVIGATING THE CAUTIOUS CIRCLE

If indeed so much annoying Thai behavior is found in circle three, then naturally everyone's goal is to place oneself in the Cautious Circle as early or as often as possible. For in this second circle, we usually get treated with the dignity we deserve.

The Thai accomplishes this through his clothing, his demeanor, an appropriate usage of language or a dignified look in order to remind others that he is not to be taken lightly.

For the foreigner, this isn't so easy. If he encounters Thais in public places, they may not always be skilled at distinguishing between foreign tourists (who are fair game) and foreign residents like us (who, one would hope, are not). Once a foreigner can succeed in being identified as a resident, he tends to get Cautious Circle treatment. By dressing well he gives the Thais a clue. By using a few Thai phrases, he gives another. For if he were just a tourist here for a few days, how could he learn to speak those words of Thai? And if he can speak a bit of Thai he may know that oranges are not fifty baht per kilo, but more like twenty. Additionally, if a foreigner can use a few Thai words and smile, the message goes forth that this foreigner wants to express good will toward the Thais, whatever circle he is operating in.

In the work place, Thais have no problem figuring out how to interact with you; they will do so with consideration, politeness and respect. It feels a lot better being treated this way than it did a few minutes ago by those motorcycle taxis. But at the same time, this is where some problems of a different kind come into play. Because in the second circle, Thais at times tend to be too cautious.

Suppose that a Thai subordinate has a fairly critical problem to discuss with you. She peeps in your room and sees you in dep concentration with that furrowed brow look of yours. Seeing how busy you are (she might not see that you are actually reading the morning cartoons) and not wishing to bother you, she decides to wait for a better opportunity. When you find out later that the problem was really quite urgent, you question the judgment of this person. You might naturally overlook the fact that she was only practicing one of the most appropriate of the Thai values.

Understanding the behavior of your staff and co-workers in terms of the values they hold dear will put them at ease, and allow you and them to develop more mutually acceptable ways of working together. Using the Thais' values yourself in your interactions will not only impress, but motivate them beyond your expectations.

The following are five of the more prominent Thai values, which contribute to establishing and maintaining relationships in the work place.

KRENG JAI

One of the most important and intriguing of Thai concepts is the term, *kreng jai* (pronounced a little like graeng jai). At one Thai university, more than a hundred master degree theses have been written by students, dealing with the useful and detrimental effects of *kreng jai* in national development. It is a significant concept not only in the abstract but also in the daily behavior of Thais, practiced by individuals from lower ranks of society all the way up to ministerial level. Of particular relevance to supervisors and managers is the use of *kreng jai* as a motivator.

Thais themselves often find it difficult to get Expatriates a complete or coherent definition of *kreng jai*. And yet the practice of *kreng jai* is found in dozens of daily situations; a term very much at the front of most Thais' minds as they try to create and nurture good human relationships. The behavior is dominant in most social relationships, and to a large extent, in work as well.

Broadly speaking, *kreng jai* refers to an attitude whereby an individual tries to restrain his own interest or desire, in situations where there is the potential for discomfort or conflict, and where there is a need to maintain a pleasant and cooperative relationship. A more complete picture is pieced together from the following examples:

1. Complying with others' wishes or requests:
Mr. A, whose car is not working properly, knows that Mrs. B lives in the same neighborhood as he does. He asks her if he can have a lift home. On this particular day, unknown to A, Mrs. B was actually planning to go shopping rather than go straight home. But, in deference or *kreng jai* to Mr. A, she cheerfully agrees to drop him at his house. She does not let A know of her previous plans.

2. Reluctance to disturb or interrupt others:
Miss M, secretary to Mr. P, has just received some important news affecting the status of Mr. P's marketing campaign. Right now Mr. P is speaking with another executive, so she refrains from interrupting him even though the delay may be crucial.

3. Restraint of one's show of displeasure or anger so as not to cause discomfort to others.
Mr. B. has been unhappy at work for some time. He decides to resign but does not trouble the boss with the actual reason.

4. Avoidance of asserting one's opinions or needs:
In a meeting to discuss plans for a staff party, Mr. D avoids putting forward his idea because he knows it runs contrary to the one held by Mrs. T. This reluctance to contradict someone else is intensified if the others have more seniority. Indeed, if D's direct superior is present, the likelihood that he will express his opinion directly is practically nil.

5. Reluctance to give instructions or pass orders to a superior, or to peers with more age or experience:
This form of *kreng jai* is often found when a younger person in an organization is promoted for reasons of competence over an older person. The younger one, who is now the boss, will show special caution and diplomacy in exercising any new authority over the elder.

Similarly, if a manager assigns a very junior person to communicate an order to a more senior department manager, that transaction will be extremely uncomfortable for the junior to carry out.

6. Reluctance to evaluate a colleague's or superior's performance.

Many companies have found it very difficult to institute a system of performance-review based on western models because of the essentially "confrontative quality" of the exercise. In the Thai tradition, the giving of criticism, even constructive criticism, has never been done directly except by a very senior to a very junior person.

7. Avoiding the demand for one's rights:

One evening Ms. G's neighbors are having a big party at their house. One of the guests' cars has been parked in front of G's gate, so G cannot get her car out. Because of kreng jai, G will choose to wait for the guest to leave rather than disturb the host (who in turn would feel kreng jai toward his own guest.)

8. Reluctance to ask questions when one has not understood someone:

When Ms. K hears an instruction, she may not ask all the necessary questions to make sure it is clear. She may ask a colleague who was nearby to explain it to her later. The reason she doesn't ask her boss may be that she doesn't want to appear ignorant, but equally likely that she doesn't want to disturb or delay him. Moreover, if the boss is a fairly intense and driven type anyway—i.e., he projects stress and impatience—her *kreng jai* is practically guaranteed.

Kreng jai Towards Juniors:

Kreng jai, in the examples given above, is practiced most commonly by juniors toward seniors—seniors with whom they have frequent contact and therefore have reason to treat with consideration and honor. But on some occasions, a senior will show *kreng jai* toward a junior. If an elderly couple have just entertained a large group of guests at home until a late hour, the hostess may tell her maids to sleep late the next morning; or she may help straighten up the living room herself. Or, coming home late from a party, the same couple may open their gate themselves rather than wake up their household staff to do it.

Variations on *Kreng Jai*:

Kreng jai, though certainly found in western societies, is probably not found to the same degree or in the same situations. But *kreng jai* as practiced by Thai people involves some discrimination in its use. For example, a person can be "too" *kreng jai* (at which point his behavior is called *khee kreng jai*, or "obsequious") or, at the other extreme, not displaying "enough" *kreng jai*, and is readily marked as such. A person may also run out of the willingness to be *kreng jai* toward someone else, especially if the latter has been repeatedly selfish, or failed to recognize or appreciate that his colleague was being *kreng jai* toward him. Such a feeling, *mot khwam kreng jai* ("*kreng jai* is finished"), is difficult if not impossible to reverse.

Kreng Jai in Government:
Kreng jai, as implied earlier, can intervene in the high levels of government. Two examples:

In recent years, efforts have been made from time to time to investigate government officials on charges of corruption. When a relative of the accused learns that one member of the investigating committee is also a relative, the investigation slows down or comes to a halt. In one such case, some of the suspected officials were of very high rank. A department regulation required that the probing committee must consist of "members of a higher or similar rank,

49

and the ministry had no official of such rank." Thus the investigation could not even get off the ground.

At high levels of government, *kreng jai* makes it difficult for a bright subordinate to contradict a director-general or minister on crucial matters of policy.

Don't *Kreng Jai* Me:

Many Thais and Expatriates who have achieved a successful two-way flow of ideas and information have done so by reducing the formality or severity they project to subordinates. They have reduced some of the gap through a continuing effort which may require weeks or months, trying to prove that they are sincerely receptive to employees' questions, opinions, objections, and even criticisms. A manager may tell his people, "You do not need to be *kreng jai* to me." He need hardly fear that his people may drop their *kreng jai* toward him altogether. As long as they have esteem for him they will continue to show him consideration in many other ways, some obvious, some less so. But over time, their use of *kreng jai* as a reason for not being open can be reduced to a level acceptable to both the Expatriate and Thai. In this way, the foreign manager has made use of the term *kreng jai* as a motivator to improve communication and trust.

HAI KIAD

A motivating value which almost every Thai seeks in his or her work is known as *kiad* – honor and respect. With the addition of the word *hai*, the value known as *hai kiad* means "to give respect or show honor". Superficially, this quality might seem no different from its western counterpart. But the expression of that respect is different in emphasis and style.

The Wai: Usually, the junior is obligated to show respect to the senior. The most common form of displaying this respect is through the *wai*, the traditional Thai greeting where the hands are brought together in a sort of prayer position at chest level or mouth level, often accompanied by a slight bow.

The junior will often *wai* the first time he greets you, and when he takes his leave. Or when he accepts something important from you, especially if it is a present or a formal award.

If you are given a wai you should generally return it. But if you are carrying a heavy briefcase, it is fine to simply nod and smile. The point is to be sure to acknowledge the wai as best you can.

> *Pu Chuai, when the Chairman leaves the building, how do I WAI him?*

Seat of Honor: "I think who you are holds a lot of weight," said one American executive. "I've participated in weddings, in roles that I would have thought should have gone to fathers and brothers instead."

If you are the head of your company or an upper level executive, you may be asked to attend the wedding or funeral ceremonies of your employees. In such cases, you might be treated with more respect and deference than what you might expect (or even think you deserve) in an equivalent situation in your own country. At the same time, as a senior person you may expect to take a role in the ceremonies themselves.

With your attendance, you are also lending to the ceremony the weight and honor of your position, which frequently creates great feelings of indebtedness in the employee concerned. It's *hai kiad* that you have offered to the event. (More examples of these roles are given in Chapter Six.)

Hai Kiad **as a Motivator:** A Thai gets the feeling of *kiad* when his boss asks his advice. He gets it when his boss introduces him to a visitor. When the boss points out a good piece of his work to someone else, or praises an idea in front of others, he is expressing *hai kiad*. When, during a meeting, a Thai colleague gives a somewhat faulty opinion, the boss will treat the Thai gently and respectfully. The elderly janitor who is no longer very efficient gains much *kiad* and satisfaction from the managing director who greets him by name and stops to chat. And he's sincere. Word gets around.

51

NAM JAI

The word *jai* means "heart". To give an indication of how much Thais are concerned with the symbolic meaning of the word, *jai* can be compounded with well over one hundred other words. A most common compound, and incidentally one of the values most prized by Thai people, is *nam jai*, or "Water from the Heart". This value is reflected in genuine acts of kindness or a voluntary extension of help, to someone you know or even a stranger, without the expectation of anything in return.

Let's say you park your car in a certain parking lot fairly often. One day, when you go back to your car you notice it has been wiped clean by someone. If the person who performed the act is nowhere to be seen, then you know you've been on the receiving end of *nam jai*. On the other hand, if the person is still hanging around your car, hinting somehow that he is responsible, this is not *nam jai*. It's five (or ten) baht he's after.

A very common form of *nam jai* is when someone brings some food into the office and lays it out on the table for everyone. Usually it is something that the person has bought back from a vaca-

tion or a business trip, to indicate that he has been thinking about his colleagues.

It can also be considered *nam jai* if you offer to help out a co-worker or subordinate who is working hard on something, perhaps working overtime. Rewarding your whole staff with a night out of food and drink after a particularly busy stretch can be an extremely good motivator, making your staff grateful for the *nam jai* you've displayed. It's not usually planned far in advance, more on the spur of the moment.

An interesting story was related by a Vietnamese manager who was supervising a team of Thai engineers trying to meet a difficult deadline. The team managed to finish the job by about 2130 hours, after the rest of the staff had gone home. Rather than have his group go their separate ways, the manager spontaneously invited everyone out for a few drinks and a meal. He was surprised, not only at the alacrity with which they agreed to go along at that late hour, but that everyone showed up promptly the next day for work, even more cheerful than before.

Nam jai is sometimes confused with *kreng jai*. Simply put, *nam jai* is a value that requires a person to take the initiative in demonstrating consideration for another. *Kreng jai* is the opposite; it usually requires a person to hold back on taking action or expressing himself.

HEN JAI

Another quality Thais admire in a good supervisor is called *hen jai*—literally, the ability to "See (into) the Heart". Such a boss has an understanding, an empathy for the subordinate, his duties and his burdens. When a boss who has this quality of *hen jai* is about to assign a task, she might take a moment to find out what other jobs the junior person is currently working on. If she sees he's overloaded, she might even reconsider the assignment. Having the quality of *hen jai* also implies the willingness to listen and perhaps to be flexible on a policy, by dealing with employees and problems on a case-by-case basis. This treatment is seen as humane, and serves very much as a motivator.

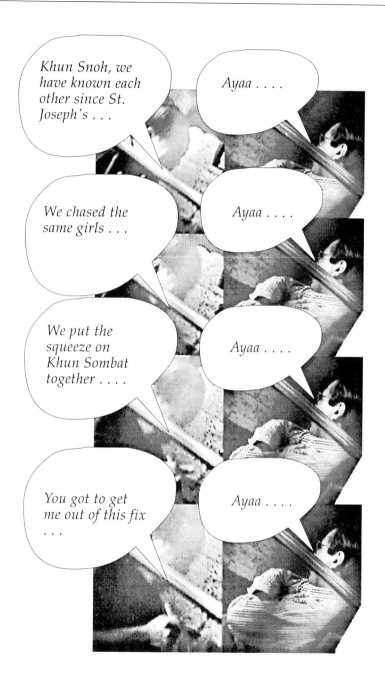

When a person has made a mistake, he is usually ashamed about it and may be afraid to discuss it with his boss. These feelings are natural with people anywhere, but are particularly acute in this hierarchal society. If the boss can put the person at ease by "looking into his heart" and indicating that she understands how the person feels, the Thai worker will certainly feel grateful for this merciful attitude. This does not mean that you should approve every mistake a person makes, but that time should be taken to give the other a chance to explain, and for you to show that you acknowledge his problems and difficulties.

> "I see what you mean. Now I understand why you had trouble the other day."

> "You're saying that no matter who you called, nobody could give you the information you needed. And that's why you're report wasn't ready for the meeting. Well, that's understandable."

> "You've moved even further out of town? And even though you wake up at 4 o'clock every morning, you can't seem to get here on time, right? You must be pretty tired when you get here."

Hen jai is a bit like empathy, but it sometimes goes one step further. In response to the circumstances, a manager may demonstrate the willingness, if necessary, to take some flexible, accommodating action on behalf of the employee. One Thai personnel manager with a Swiss multi-national offered her opinion:

> For some companies, it's very clear. No work, no pay, right? If you are six months sick and you cannot work, you get a lump sum payment of six months and you're finished. Here we have that kind of rule too, but when we try to implement it, it's not that easy. We really have to think. This guy is very young and he has two kids. His wife doesn't work. It means that if you let him go today, he'll be in big trouble tomorrow. So in this case we cannot really follow the rule.

SAM RUAM

> It's important not to show your anger. Thais are very sensitive to emotion and feel very uncomfortable about the nature of anger. Even if it is anger directed towards a situation, Thais might interpret it as anger directed toward them.

> When I get angry, I get very quiet. I don't say anything. When I'm upset with something my boss said, I just say, "Okay, I understand," and then I walk out. After a few days we can talk more rationally about the situation. Thais don't like confrontation.
>
> —Thai manager in an American multinational

Thais are taught from a young age that one should strive to exercise restraint and maintain composure in stressful situations, avoiding extreme displays of emotion, whether one is angry, sad—or even happy. This value is called *sam ruam*, related to a Buddhist concept of moderation, "to travel the middle path".

Anger: It is difficult to generalize, of course, about how people express their anger. Many of us might get upset at our office colleague in one way, at our boss in another way, and at our spouse in yet another manner. But Thais generally claim that Westerners tend to show their anger with stretched or distorted facial lines, heightened skin color, and a louder voice. The degree of expression will vary according to culture and personal style. The Thai might occasionally see the odd Expatriate bang his fist on the table. In short, when a Westerner loses his temper the signals are more visible—i.e., it's "louder".

Among Thais in the Cautious Circle— e.g., at their place of work—they too can get angry, but their depiction of anger is very different. The angry Thai becomes subdued. His skin may actually grow paler, the facial muscles may tighten slightly. He may take a deep, rather impressive breath. And his voice and gestures are softer than normal. It is this ability to mute the outward signs of anger that marks a Thai person of good upbringing; the more senior he is, the more others expect such self-control. Furthermore, this quiet show of anger has frequently, in fact, awesome impact on subordinates; it really gets results. Should a senior person have an outburst of temper he cannot control, subordinates may be distracted from his point by the "noise", or worse, may lose some respect for him. He can't manage himself.

Another dimension of anger is *how long it will last*. Many Westerners claim that their anger is short-lived. Several Australians have told us that, "we might blow our top at you at three in the after-

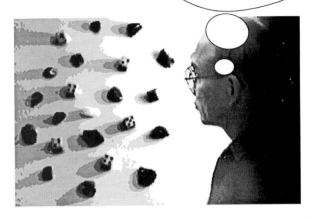

*Let's see,
over the past 15 years
I've worked with nine
Expats – no wonder
I'm losing my hair . . .*

noon and invite you for a beer at five." Thais, whose anger generally appears to last longer, might take some comfort in knowing that they often attach much greater weight and concern to Westerners' loss of temper than do the Westerners themselves. And Expats can see that in view of the foregoing remarks, the way they "manage their anger" matters a lot to Thais.

Frustration: The show by foreigners of frustration is frequently confused by Thais for a show of anger. How often has an Expat manager been told by his Thai secretary that a client's telephone is still engaged, or worse, out of order. His "Good God! Again?"—or more colorful outbursts—are really directed only at the "system," not at the person standing in front of him. But the outburst is likely to be taken personally by the secretary, who feels he is blaming her for the problem.

Happiness: A common case of confusion for foreigners in Thailand is the expression of gratitude by Thais. In everyday Western practice, we see the expression "thank you" spoken quite clearly, even at times profusely. In some western countries, after a dinner party a well-mannered guest emphasizes her gratitude even further—again explicitly—by means of a telephone call to the hostess or a thank-you note.

What? You already sold that house?

What can I do now? I promised the house to John!

Ok. I'll tell him the house burned down.

Such practices are pretty rare among Thais. Often "thanks" are given by means of a *wai*, the graceful and respectful gesture well known to visitors. A good case in point appears when a Thai gives another Thai a wedding present. The receiver takes the gift with a *wai* and sets it aside without opening it. Then without commenting further on the gift, she may ask the giver two or three seemingly irrelevant questions about his journey through traffic, how his relatives are—all questions focused on the giver rather than the gift.

Is the Thai lady who received the gift keen to know what's inside the wrapper?

You bet.

But she has been taught that this is one event where restraint and composure are required. Extremes of emotion—either negative or positive—should be moderated; being excessively verbal in praise of a gift would show, according to Buddhist guidelines, that her desires for material things have got the better of her.

When the guest is gone, she'll have a look.

A more relevant case in point might occur when the foreign manager gives an important promotion to a subordinate. According to Thai rules of decorum, the subordinate may express his delight with such restraint and subtlety that the boss may seriously wonder if the raise was sufficient.

Sadness: Self-control in cases of grief or remorse are also expected of the good Buddhist Thai. At a funeral, where Westerners might expect to see tears, they are more likely to see stoicism. As one Thai father wrote in regards to his daughter's ideal comportment, "If someone close to her should die, she is not supposed to weep or moan about it, but rather to keep her feelings to herself. After all, they are *her* feelings, and she should not inflict them on others."

When I'm big,
I'll have
PHRADET like
him –
I hope . . .

FOUR

Some Key Thai Concepts of Management

You have to do three things to succeed as a manager in Thailand:

1) You have to earn their friendship, in order to get their trust;

2) You have to earn their respect. In order to earn their respect you have to be in a position of seniority or you have to command fear resulting from your power;

3) And you have to make them owe you something. Always give and make them see that you are always sacrificing and giving. Then they'll always think that their boss is very giving and sincere.

Your staff will be fearful of you, but they will also be obligated to you. And then they will do everything for you.

– Thai hotel manager

THE NATURAL ORDER OF THINGS

The concepts expressed here might suggest that this Thai has been somewhat influenced by the Machiavelli School of Management. But there's accuracy and realism in what she says. On the other hand, lest you think she is very mechanistic, her behavior, as interpreted by her subordinates, is quite warm, friendly, humane, and completely genuine.

Most Thais are reasonably comfortable with the notion that some individuals in society "deserve" to have power. As mentioned earlier, many Thais believe that the person with power gained it, at least to some extent, through the accumulation of merit in earlier existences. The society is therefore ranked—a natural order of things. This acceptance of power is easiest for Thai subordinates when the manager (male or female) is already in place, with his or her rank already designated. On the other hand, when a Thai becomes a manager by emerging through the ranks, it is much more difficult for him to assume acceptable or credible power.

A foreign manager is accorded a considerable degree of "automatic" respect; Thais tend to accept his power and authority as "given". By virtue of his having come from overseas and the home office, they see him as having a certain additional amount of power and credibility not possessed by a Thai. He is seen, so to speak, as "the Company" itself, like one of the owners. This feeling, coupled with a certain admiration (quite often exaggerated) for "foreign" things and skills, gives the Expat manager an aura of authority, right from the start.

Over the centuries, the kings of Thailand have been feared and adored. Thais have grown to expect a leader to demonstrate a blend of authoritarianism and benevolence. Accordingly, many Thai politicians, civil servants, and corporate executives still model their leadership in the royal mold.

The two fibers woven into the leader's mantle are called *phradet*, "the traditional exercise of authority and toughness", and *phrakhun*, "the traditional system of patronization".

PHRADET

What are some of the ways in which power should be exercised by a senior Thai? We speak here of an ideal Thai boss. This ideal is distinct from certain local bullies (known as *nak laeng* in Thai), and corrupt military or political figures, who are held more in awe than admiration because of their abuses of power.

Decision-making: The boss is expected to decide things. Since he has qualified as a boss, it is assumed that he possesses certain knowledge, wisdom, or experience which go beyond the capacity of his colleagues. Most of the problems, in the traditional Thai system (most exemplified in the bureaucracy), are passed up the line for the most senior person to decide upon. It would be fair to describe this system as "upward" delegation. The result, of course, is a buildup of a myriad of major and minor decisions on the top person's desk.

Decisions in "Thai" companies are not usually made as a "team", as is frequently done in Japan or certain western countries. It might be surprising to learn that, according to a recent study, Thais found it perfectly acceptable for a Thai boss to decide things in (as they put it) an "authoritarian" way. They made it clear, though, that an authoritarian boss should nevertheless ask for subordinates' opinions. But once having done so, he is perfectly entitled to do what he thinks is correct as it is his job to decide. What is not very acceptable, however, is the "dictatorial" manager (*phu phadetkan*), who decides without consulting anyone. There is a very thin line in the distinction between authoritarian and dictatorial, but most Thais seem to regard one key courtesy from the boss as essential, namely that he or she should show an interest in their views.

Mr. (or Ms.) Know-it-All: The Thai manager holds a greater percentage of the organization's power and decision-making authority than most of his western counterparts. He is also expected to be knowledgeable in virtually all the aspects of business departments over which he supervises. This Thai feeling, that a manager needs to have complete expertise, is an important difference from the popular western notion. Many Europeans, for example, feel that the manager should employ experts to work for him; he doesn't have to be an expert himself in each of their fields. And then he delegates.

PHRAKHUN

Head of the Family: If the Thai manager holds considerable power, he also feels that he must carry a greater degree of responsibility for the personal lives of his constituents than does his western counterpart. He is seen, to some extent, as a father figure.

Having authority entails a set of duties. If a Thai becomes rich and powerful, he takes on certain paternal and patron-like roles, both towards less fortunate relatives, and to junior members of his work entourage. If he has a poor cousin working as a housemaid, for example, he would have to make sure that she does not have to continue working at that job once he himself has become an important person; if he neglected such a duty, other relatives would think him selfish. As for his junior work colleagues, he'd be expected to protect them, somewhat as he would care for family members, take an interest in their personal welfare and family life. All this is a way of showing his recognition for their supporting roles in his meteoric rise. It is the kind of behavior, as the Thai hotel manager explains, which contributes to the bonding process.

Many Thai managers would feel reasonably comfortable discussing employees' personal lives with them, to the extent that what was happening at home seemed to affect their work. According to some Western managers, this would be an unacceptable invasion of privacy.

Noi's a problem, but I must protect her. I'm her Phu Yai.

A traditional senior Thai could expect to be approached from time to time by relatives and former clients to help get them jobs. Once they are on board he would be rather considerate of them. If they did poorly he might try to protect them, at least for a while.

ENGENDERING LOYALTY

The Thai boss, as stated before in Chapter Two, is like a father to his subordinates. He will take them to task and work them hard, but he will also cover their mistakes, reward them lavishly, and help manage their personal affairs from hospital bills to education costs to funerals. Doing good deeds for one's subordinates builds up a boss' store of goodwill, or *bunkhun*, the value explained in the previous chapter. Such a reserve is a boss' invaluable resource, for the other side of this coin is that his juniors or subordinates feel a certain obligation to him, or *katanyu*, and expect to provide certain duties and services to him.

It is easier to appreciate this system especially since the "State" hasn't in the past done very much in the way of welfare, insurance, or social security, and it has always been up to the family or the work group (especially its head person) to take care of the needs of the group members. Indeed, one who emerges as the top person has done so in part because he fulfills both leadership roles—exercising power, while giving benevolence to his constituents. A premium, therefore, is placed on his skills of attracting, deploying and looking after people. The senior person is often a master of building and nurturing human relationships, both within his group, and with outside power sources as well.

The effective supervisor treats his Thai colleagues (including domestic staff) a little like "respected relatives." Between a Thai supervisor and his staff, even the pronouns they use reflect this relationship. There is mutual concern for personal problems as well as professional matters.

Thais who serve today as leaders in the formal structure are still expected to behave in some of these traditional ways, even though the modern systems of companies like ESSO and IBM have taken over many of the old personnel support functions once provided

PHRADET—PHRAKHUN
The Traditional Thai Model
of Effective Leadership

PHRADET	PHRAKHUN
Traditional Exercise of Authority and Toughness	Traditional System of Patronization
- Delegate tasks and authority	- Give money, shelter, food clothing
- Demand loyalty	- Give care during sickness or other crisis
- Demand that work be done	- Give protection vis-a-vis outsiders
- Dispense justice	- Lend prestige (prestige from affiliations)
- Administer discipline or punishment	- Sponsorship: education, marriage, ordination, funeral etc.
- Play a mediating role	- Give rewards
- Exercise firmness	- All of the above extended to members of the subordinate's family.
- Make policies	
- Introduce improvement	

in a more personal way. Non-Thai managers, too, will be appreciated if they are able to play some of these father-figure roles, while maintaining the even-handedness that they are much admired for. These efforts can actually lead to constitute a measure of *bunkhun* for them, even in a relatively short period.

BARAMEE

Exercising a balance between these two factors, *phradet* and *phrakhun*, over a period of time gives a leader *baramee*—power and strength derived from respect and loyalty.

Having *baramee* enables a person to exercise influence, protect his people, and command obedience and loyalty from others, so he can accomplish most of what he sets out to achieve. *Baramee* is both a cause and effect, a result of past deeds which generate further potential. Furthermore, if a person possesses it, the baramee will also extend to those who are related or affiliated to him.

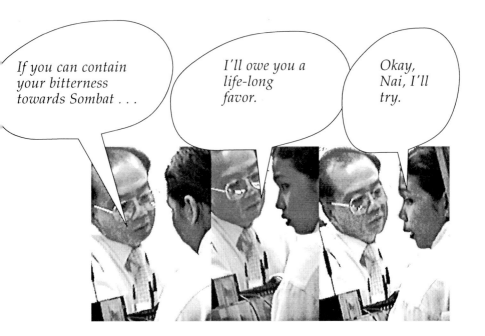

> *If you can contain your bitterness towards Sombat . . .*

> *I'll owe you a life-long favor.*

> *Okay, Nai, I'll try.*

Some day in the office, you might be surprised to hear one of your senior Thai colleagues is scolding a subordinate with a complete lack of restraint; it sounds like a real "dressing down." You are perplexed since this is not at all the type of behavior you understood was proper in this culture. If you look more closely into this relationship, however, you will probably discover that the senior Thai has accumulated a considerable store of *bunkhun* with that subordinate over the years, to the point where you could say he possesses *baramee*. Simply put, the boss who has developed deep and trusting relationships with his subordinates can manage to break the standard rules of office etiquette and be forgiven.

Who? Me? A father figure?

I've got
a better
plan . . .

. . . but can
I explain it
well enough?

Is my
English up
to it?

Better
not risk
it.

FIVE

Getting the Job Done

As was seen in the previous three chapters, Thais operate within a hierarchical system of relationships, can intuitively move horizontally from Family Circle to Cautious Circle, and on to the Selfish Circle and back, and tend to be receptive to "father-figure" type bosses in the work-place.

This, of course, is a generalization of the average Thai, and you are certainly going to meet flamboyant Thai workers in the "cautious" office, as well as perfect strangers out in the "selfish" circle who will come to your aid when you most need it and least expect it. However, understanding these qualities of the average Thai will give you the tools to *rationalize* why your Thai colleagues, subordinates, or even bosses, behave the way they do in certain situations. You will be more confident in approaching certain tasks as a manager in Thailand with greater cultural sensitivity and skill, and this will help you get the job done.

Some of the tasks:

Motivating Thais: "How can I make them happy and productive?"

Creating a Sense of Urgency and Respect for Deadlines: "Where is that bloody report?"

Delegation and Accountability: "Don't Thais want to take responsibility?"

Encouraging Initiative: "Do I have to tell them to do everything?"

Facilitating Better Communication: "How do I know if they understand, and how can they make me realize that they don't understand?"

Evaluation, Criticism and Discipline: "Why can't I just tell it the way it is?"

Fostering Teamwork Among Departments: "Why can't we all work together? Aren't we all working for the same company?"

Dealing With Government: "What are we supposed to be paying them taxes for?"

MOTIVATING THAIS

How do you motivate the Thais? How do you motivate anyone? It is very difficult to generalize about something so individual and complex as what motivates people, and this is equally true in describing the Thai. *Money* may be the most important factor to a college graduate, but may be somewhat irrelevant to an executive who comes from a wealthy background. A Thai-Chinese may take to

your management-by-objective style like fish to water, but a more traditional Thai may struggle to stay afloat in such a high-pressure atmosphere.

However, of the many factors that can influence particular individuals in the Thai work force, five are especially significant among a wide range of people. Those factors are: money, security, company image, personal prestige and workplace atmosphere.

MONEY

There is no question that today's leading motivator is *money*. In a recent survey of Chulalongkorn University Faculty of Arts students, over twenty-five percent of some 450 students surveyed said they felt a monthly salary of Baht 20 to 30,000 would be reasonable to expect. Although they are students from what is considered the most prestigious university in Thailand, as Faculty of Arts students they are probably aiming thirty to fifty percent higher than what they are actually going to get .

However, what many of these students will learn is that there aren't enough skilled people to fill the growing number of specialized positions. So once they get into the work force and develop a marketable expertise (engineering, accounting, training, personnel systems, sales, language, computers, etc.) they may be able to hop from company to company, doubling their wages as they go.

> One of our staff was working the time-keeping box before he was moved into the restaurant service as a busboy. He's been, I think, working as a busboy for five or six months, and he's leaving tomorrow. He's moving to another hotel. As a result, in less than a year, he's probably increased his salary by more than double, from Baht 3,500 to Baht 7,000. At our hotel you develop some skills within the industry and you can move on to the next level. Finally you may be able to reach the dizzy heights of the Grand Hyatt, or the Regent.
> — Australian business hotel manager

SECURITY

Traditionally, in a successful Thai work group, there was a strong bond between boss and worker, a personal bond of loyalty to the person rather than the institution he works for. It was common to hear that when a popular department manager decided to quit his organization, his whole team (called *phak-phuak*) would go with him. This exodus would frequently have no relation to salaries and benefits.

In recent years, as the Thai economy has accelerated, salary and promotion factors have become more significant. But in spite of this shift in work values and priorities, the loyalty factor is still strong. Work groups still occasionally leave en bloc. Some multinational companies haven't done all they could to nurture loyalty among employees. One difficult problem for some is that their business may be cyclical or that the shareholders demand short-term profits every quarter. The consequence, in certain cases, is that the company may decide to let staff go.

> In my company a few years ago we laid off quite a lot of workers, due to a down turn in the business. I was surprised, a few weeks later, that two of my better managers came in and said they were planning to resign! When I asked them why, one said "Well, yesterday you let a hundred workers go. Maybe next time the company may need to let *us* go too."
> — American manager, electronics firm

As things turned out, the manager did lose those individuals. But a few years later when the company ran into another bad stretch, he took an entirely different approach. Luckily, he was able to reduce working hours a certain percentage and keep everyone. This time nobody resigned, and morale and loyalty were visibly improved, quite clearly a direct result of the manager's approach to this crisis.

A second related issue is the stress often placed by multinationals on competence as compared with loyalty as a criterion for promotion or even retention. Thais generally recognize the need for competence, but feel that seniority should be valued too. Many believe that a person who has been around for years can be trusted to protect his boss, the company, and precious company information. One senior and highly competent Thai manager claimed:

> Some older employees may actually resign from a multinational and go into government service, for fear a newly-arrived farang manager will perceive them as inefficient and fire them. Some multinationals are indifferent to loyalty; they have no memory.

COMPANY IMAGE

Employees at all levels are affected by the apparent health and future prospects of the company, this "family" they have opted to work for. They want to feel that the company is viable, that it is likely to have a long and healthy life in Thailand.

If the company has great strengths back home and in other countries, the staff need and want to hear about these things. Salaried staff also want to know that their company has first rate systems and/or technology, which will give them a chance to learn new concepts and skills.

The company needs to be seen as "sincere" — a Thai word carrying a slightly different meaning from its western definition — meaning policies are strong on pay, welfare, and work stability. These policies, as well as goals, events, or changes of direction should be conveyed clearly by the head of the company. Related to the Thai concept of manager as "head of the family," many workers respond to an MD who is friendly, visible, and shows he's trying to look after their interests. That's "sincerity". Several times a year, it's useful for the top person to appear in front of the entire work force, tell the employees what's happening with the company (through an interpreter, if necessary), and answer questions in a helpful way.

Most Thais at the managerial level like to be able to see a career path and a chance for advancement. The path should be based on merit, but loyalty should also be acknowledged. Some Thais may feel there is a ceiling, above which only foreigners will be considered. It should be made clear how high a Thai can climb within the company.

If the company is strong on training, this should be greatly emphasized as Thais place strong value on education and skill development. Overseas training in particular is highly coveted, not only for self-improvement, or for the *sanuk*, or "fun" inherent in the junket, but also because of the prestige it carries in the eyes of others, inside and outside the company.

PERSONAL PRESTIGE

For some Thais, particularly the wealthier ones within your management ranks, money is not so important as personal prestige. The image of the company he works for is very important. The more spacious the office, the nicer the car and the larger the staff that reports to him, the greater the prestige. Even the wording of the worker's position within the company is sensitive and significant.

Recently, a European oil company with operations in Thailand began to notice higher turnover at the middle level. It turned out that many of these individuals had former classmates now working for Thai companies, who were enjoying the title of "manager," while they themselves (for whom salary was no problem) had no such title. When the Expat MD asked London to enlarge his roster of "manager" titles, he was initially rebuffed because the organization allotted only a limited number of managerial positions to each overseas operation. Lobbying hard, the MD eventually prevailed and got the extra slots. The result? Turnover returned to normal levels. No increases in salary were necessary. The prestige of a title, a badge which Thais wear in social circles as well as their business associations, was the missing motivator.

He's a great worker, pretty loyal . . .

but I couldn't persuade him to hang on.

They made him a manager . . . AND they doubled his salary.

MORE GAN ENG, LESS GUNG HO

I come from New York. I am a type-A person, so when I get going, I get going. I don't need a cup of coffee to get me up in the morning. I get to the office at 0630. I work twelve, thirteen hours straight. I take a break for lunch of course, but I just work it hard. (The Thais) sometimes seem to lack that zeal, that passion, that drive. They're more laid back. I wish they were more productive. They talk a lot, they joke a lot, they kid a lot, they eat a lot. They turn the work out, but not like if I had twelve Harry Michaelses*—Yeah, I think we'd be doing thirty to forty percent more work. Now that would be strictly on a productivity basis. I don't want to say their quality's better than mine, or mine is better than theirs; but there would just be more of the work.

—American Manager, manufacturing firm

The ultimate Thai workplace (according to many Thais) is where he or she feels at home. After all, she's going to see more of her boss and co-workers in a given week than she is her own family and friends . In fact, she may spurn other higher-paying offers from other companies if she considers the people she works with as "family" or friends. They are people she enjoys chatting with, having meals with, taking trips with, and working hard with. To have an office that operates like one big, happy family is to have *gan eng*, "a pleasant, friendly atmosphere", where people feel at home.

Unfortunately for Thais, they often have to deal with the Harry Michaelses of the world, people who are driving their hardest to implement proven management systems and concepts, but sometimes end up "turning off" their staff. If they don't discover the right balance of Western and Thai management, they often get labeled with the Thai epithet, "He's too serious".

Foreigners can be too serious. That means they are always working. They want to finish the job. No time to smile. No time to say hello. No time to say, "How's your kid?" Thais, we are also working, but we are working towards having good relationships. We try to show that we care about others, that we are concerned about their families or their friends.

—Thai manager, American airline firm

---

* Not his real name

An Australian hotel manager with over a decade of experience in managing Thais put it more bluntly:

> Do you know anything about your Thai staff? Do you know where they come from? Do you know what they want out of life? Do you know what they want to do in the future? Do you know how many girlfriends they have? You should, if you don't. Because I think that's an important part of dealing with human beings in general, but with Thais, the family thing must be touched upon more than occasionally. I'm not saying you have to spend your entire time talking with them about their private lives, but you've got to let them know that you care about them to a certain degree. They're not going to get a report out by Monday for you or give you that extra effort, because you don't care about them, do you? You only care about your bloody report.

A SENSE OF URGENCY AND RESPECT FOR DEADLINES

> When I first arrived from Europe, I came here with the belief that you go to work eight hours a day, you get certain tasks to complete and you are expected to complete these tasks within a certain deadline. If you don't complete these tasks within the deadline, there must be consequences if you don't have a reason why they aren't completed. And the main problem here in Thailand was that the Thais didn't react the way I expected. When a deadline was given, deadlines were not kept.
>
> — Danish executive, transport firm

URGENCY, THAI AND NON-THAI STYLE

It is in the areas of planning and deadlines where the Thai desire for *gan eng* comes into conflict with the industrialized world's drive for precision and urgency.

Work is treated in the West as a continuous series of inter-related activities; one segment leads to the next step, and so forth. The preferred work pattern is steady, even relentless. There's a great concern for planning, to assure this developmental build-ing process and achieve goals a year or five years hence. The future is seen, to some extent, as being predictable, even con-trollable.

The Thai norm in this respect tends to be different. Many Thais do not always perceive the same connection as Europeans do between certain individual tasks. Nor is the future so reliable. This partly explains a certain lack of enthusiasm for making projections and monitoring goals along a schedule. In what was, for centuries, an agricultural society, it just wasn't necessary. Like farmers who work within agricultural cycles, urban Thais tackle tasks more in bursts than as a steady stream. Projects are often completed in a flurry of last minute effort. And afterward it makes sense to relax a bit in between jobs.

MEETING QUOTAS AND DEADLINES

When some supervisors give a work assignment they say, "Your quota is five hundred widgets this month," or "I want the living room cleaned by 1600." This could be described as the "push" technique.

In view of Thais' penchant for participating and being given some room for independence, some managers recommend a "pull" rather than a "push" approach. According to this technique, the boss might ask, "How much of our overall goal for the year of three thousand widgets do you think you can do this month?" One such manager, following this method, thinks "The Thai will estimate three or four hundred (remember, he wants his options), and eventually do five hundred that month." He is likely to perform better if he has helped to set the target.

INSTILLING A SENSE OF URGENCY

Getting commitment to urgency can sometimes be more than a little frustrating. A few guidelines may be helpful.

One should take extra time to explain the reason for urgency concerning the matter at hand. Stressing the consequences of not getting the job done on time tends to be a very effective motivator. Often enough, your colleagues have never been fully told how the job fits into a chain of events, ending up with a customer who simply won't want the product after the first of May.

In some cases, a personal appeal can help. "I'm afraid I will be in trouble with *my* boss if we don't get this shipment out." If the staff members like you, they will value and want to protect your relationships with your superiors.

Frequent follow-up is essential, especially if it's a new or unfamiliar project. And if you can word your request in a supportive manner, without applying too much intense pressure, it helps.

DELEGATION AND ACCOUNTABILITY

It's the beginning of the year and we've just had approval for the annual salary increases. I've "empowered" all our heads of departments to take the approved budget and come back with a proposal for salary increases based on performance over the past twelve-month period. The first department head, who had only one staff member to evaluate, came back to me today, showed me the blank sheet and said, "How much do you think I should give him"? His question defeats the whole purpose of delegation. It's not as if they come in and say, "I don't think we should make this decision." I think it's because they're scared. They're not used to making those kind of power-assuming decisions.

—Australian hotel manager

DIFFERENT VIEWS OF DELEGATION AND ACCOUNTABILITY

As seen in the previous chapter, traditional Thai "heads of family" companies often operate under the concept of *Phradet*, an authoritarian model of management. In Thailand, where organizations commonly had employees of widely different social and educational levels, managers had lower levels of confidence in their subordinates' capacity for leadership and initiative. Furthermore, many Thai managers (often schooled in Chinese-style family business) do not favor the sharing of information with subordinates nor involving them in decision-making.*

---

* Redding, 1976

These factors all contribute to a lower trust in delegation as a management tool. Indeed, a Thai friend of ours went one step further with his own view: "If my boss delegates a lot, I think he's basically lazy."

Another factor may be that the collectivist, agrarian values did not require the idea of accountability in the individual sense. As one American managing director with seven years' experience in Thailand said, "It's just a different approach. In the U.S. people see themselves as individuals and you can give them individual assignments. Here, the Thais work within the context of the group where responsibilities are shared. If you give them individual responsibilities with individual accountabilities, it runs up against their grain."

The consequence for the Thai subordinate is that when he is delegated work, he will probably work at it diligently; however, he doesn't feel the full weight of responsibility over the outcome of the assignment. He also doesn't feel the need to give an account of his actions to his boss, partly because it's his boss' job to know without being told! In his mind, he will have done the job exactly as he was told. If the result does not turn out favorably, then it is not his fault — it's the boss' fault for not delegating properly!

KEEPING AN EYE ON THINGS

One manager calls it micro-managing. Another calls it upward delegation by the subordinates. No matter how it's described, the word "delegation" assumes a different connotation when adapted to managing in Thailand. It tends to increase, not decrease, the manager's workload. However, delegation is possible.

My advice to newly arrived Expats would be one hundred percent delegate, don't abdicate. And I mean, don't "abdicate"! Even if you perceive yourself to be the general, you have to manage like you're still the "captain". The general sets policy, direction and overall strategy. He then passes that down to the captain who has an organizational responsibility to get done what the person above him has instructed him to do. The Expatriate manager in Thailand has got to have both the attitude of the general, but maintain the responsibilities of the captain.

— American hotel executive

A Western or Japanese manager would expect his delegated subordinate to make an account of his assignment with progress reports, explanations or questions. The Thai manager would probably not expect such accounting, at least not to the Western degree. Thus, the Expat manager has to be on his toes if he wants to keep himself in the picture.

"Lek, how's the project going? Can I see what you've done? What's going on with this?" I think my mind has developed what you might call a Rolodex. I delegate a project and three days later little cards pop up in my head with little notes that say, "How are the billboard photos going? Mali, what about the security program? Somchai, did you get the parts that you need?" It's one right after the other. Some people might construe that as micro-managing. But for the most part, it's very difficult to be a hands-off manager here, except perhaps when dealing with the rare overseas-educated Thai managers.
— American executive, airline firm

81

THE WEIGHT OF RESPONSIBILITY

The managing director quoted above feels tremendous pressure in keeping track of all the projects and assignments his subordinates are working on. And yet, for the most part, he feels frustrated in making his people take responsibility. Even in cases where the Thais feel there is a strong need for a certain policy change, they may want the boss to dictate and implement that change. The same managing director had this revealing case to relate:

> Basically, I've been the one setting prices in the market place. And I price us very expensively. In a marketing conference the other day, I again got complaints from the reps that our prices are too expensive. Here we go. It's MBO time. Western concept. I said to my sales manager and the sales reps, "I'll tell you what. You people can determine the price. You can sell it at whatever you want in the market. No problem. Just make sure we meet this forecast. And I'm not going to have any say and I'll let you change the prices over the year which means you're going to have to meet on a frequent basis, get our competitive price in position, and then change the prices accordingly. But what comes with that is, you and your sales team are completely accountable for the results. We have these objectives and if we don't meet these objectives, then you'll have to talk about it and take corrective action."

> Now, until that point, I was basically the one accountable for our sales performance because I was the one setting the prices. Yesterday, my sales manager Mali comes to see me. I say, "Mali, you haven't changed the prices at all. All I've been hearing for the past year is that we're 'too expensive'. I expected a great drop in price, you know, to meet the forecast." She replies, "Well, I think the sales team is a little reluctant. We would rather have you set the price." And I say, "I think what you're saying is that you'd rather have me accountable."

In this case, the managing director feels that he made a tactical mistake. He said that during their next meeting he would like to emphasize not their responsibility, but the company's responsibility; not the risk to the sales reps, but the risk to the company, and ultimately to the boss. After all, if the boss fails, it reflects on the entire group.

> When I go back I'll say, "Look, we are all responsible for what this station is capable of producing, what this station ultimately produces. I have my goal

and you people have to help me accomplish that goal. And then what I'm going to do is — since you people are out on the streets, you people know what we really need to do — I'm going to let you help me make that decision. So ultimately it's not going to be you, your sales team that is held accountable whether or not we meet our objectives. We are all accountable whether or not we meet our station objectives. Which means if *we* don't meet our objectives, *I'm* in trouble.

INITIATIVE

I send my people to a computer course, but once again, they don't learn what I need them to learn. They come back here and we give them an exercise, and I say, "Look, I want you to produce a project schedule," and they look blankly at me. They didn't learn that particular application. If they had gone to school and said to themselves, "OK, this is what we're doing in our office. Now can we learn more about this?" Or "How about with Word Perfect? I want to turn out columns and I want to add it up. I've got to create a system and format, but I want it with the bells and whistles." I don't know how to put the bells and whistles on. But I expect my staff, if they don't know, to find out. I'll send them to school but they'll come back having learned only lessons 1 to 10, and not ask the relevant day-to-day questions of what we actually need in our office, and the implications. If you don't know, you find out. Learn, make yourself conversant, and show me what it can do. But it doesn't happen.

– Australian executive, design firm

THE EFFECT OF OTHERS: SHOULD I VENTURE MY IDEA?

The Japanese call it *kaizen*, "continual improvement". The *kaizen* system empowers the employee to initiate measures to improve the way he does his work, particularly if the improvement also benefits the entire company. Americans used to call it Yankee Ingenuity, or the belief that any Joe can take an idea and turn it into a problem-solver or a breakthrough in industry. A productive company can no longer rely on the "genius" of one or two superstars. It needs the efforts of every single employee. One never knows where the next brilliant idea will come from. And the more people in a company striving to find it, the better chance it will happen.

The Thai culture does not encourage all its people to dare, to make mistakes, to take initiative. It encourages only a few at the top.

As seen in the previous section on delegation, when action is to be initiated — a project undertaken or a new idea proposed — Thais have traditionally believed that it's the boss who is supposed to initiate it. In keeping with the downward path of communication, it is the boss' role — not his subordinates' — to come up with proposals. Not to say that an effective boss can't encourage juniors to take initiative, but this often takes time; the first assumption by most Thais is that taking initiative is one of the responsibilities a boss is paid for.

Bosses aren't the only inhibition to initiative. It is frequently other co-workers who somehow exert a subtle form of peer pressure. Just as an excellent speaker of English may purposely try to cover up his fluency in front of other less fluent Thais, a person with a good idea may hold back on an initiative so as not to appear that he's trying to grab the spotlight.

I think Thais are scared to give any ideas, or to take responsibility. Sometimes you know it's going to be good, but you may be afraid that it's a stupid idea to others, so you're too embarrassed. That's why there's no initiative. How other people think. How other people look at you. People are too afraid. Even me.

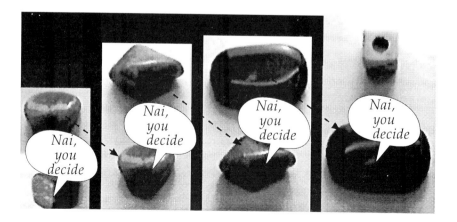

For example, yesterday, I issued a memo thanking our employees and giving them an additional two days of vacation if they had perfect attendance. "1993 was a very difficult year for all of us, so I want to thank all of you, blah, blah, blah." And I sent it to him (the managing director) to sign. After all, I had to get his approval. And he sent it back to me and approved it. He agreed with me because not too many people would get the vacation days anyway. And it's good for morale. "Okay, you do it," he said. So I rewrote the memo and wrote his name and sent it to him. He sent it back and told me to change it to my name. And I said, "No, *you* sign it." I didn't want to sign it because I was afraid of what the other department managers would think of me. "Oh, she thinks she's a big potato" or something like that.

— Thai manager, American airline firm

Two ways can help to try to overcome this cultural barrier. One is by encouraging them to speak out without fear of being ridiculed by people of authority. The faster you can encourage a "Don't *kreng jai* me" work atmosphere, and the more you reward assertiveness, the more people may develop the courage to venture new ideas.

The second thing the the Expat manager can do is some extra-curricular coaching to help them overcome their fear.

When I came here this time I didn't know anything about computers. I wanted to computerize my office, and I was concerned that in doing so I'd lose staff. I thought they might not want to go through this traumatic process of learning how to use computers. And so what I did was, we all together with the staff and my wife went to computer school. And we all learned how to do this stuff. We all went through the same frustrations, but we all had fun doing it. When we got back, we only had one computer in our office. Well, our computer turned out to be a status symbol, in addition to being very useful. Everyone wanted their own computer. Pretty soon, everyone had their own computer. Right now, some of us have two.

— American Old-hand in Thailand

Does an Expat manager have the time to coach his staff on the myriad number of tasks that they need to master? Probably not. But finding some time may inspire your staff's confidence, and just may encourage them to take the initiative and to make that extra effort to figure things out on their own. Personal coaching is a very effective motivator.

ANALYTICAL THINKING

Many Europeans have observed among Thais a lack of experience in western-style analytical thought. People brought up within a hierarchal social system are discouraged from asking the question "Why" or "Why not?" — as in "Why aren't I richer?" or "Why can't I get the pretty girl?" or "Why can't we do this job a different way?" In the agricultural environment where things don't change much from year to year, many of life's major events tended to be unchanging, predictable, and not much subject to human influence; one would basically take life as it came, and do things the way they've always been done. In such an environment, many would consider that asking a lot of "why's" would be somewhat irrelevant.

For the Westerner, of course, asking "why" is one of the keys to understanding a situation and forging ahead.

> Thai people will say, "Let's do it the same way." They will copy the precedent. They don't strive to improve. They fill out the forms they've used for years even though the forms are wrong. So now we've got to sit down and discuss the fundamentals. We've got to start asking ourselves "Why?" "Why did the 1992 sales go up? Why did those categories go down?" Keep asking until you can't go further—until you know *why*.
>
> – American manager, manufacturing firm

Westerners generally believe that systematic analytical thinking leads rather clearly to the action that should be taken. If we can't logically piece a problem together with the right questions, then how could we possibly come up with the initiative for a solution ?

The Thai educational system has traditionally stressed copying. Most students are still expected to listen to information, and then get it right on the test. Interestingly, the skills of copying have led to several thriving industries imitating other companies' products. Except for a few innovative schools, most of them attached to universities, there has been little encouragement for independent enquiry or initiative. Copying effectively, we can assume, is a necessary and useful stage which will lead to innovation a little further down the road.

Thais do practice analytical thinking especially in the area of "human relations". In this aspect of "analytical thinking" as well as planning, Thais may be far more "advanced" than other countries. The challenge lies in applying the same wealth of skills to "industrial" problems.

Since subordinates have always expected the boss to take the initiative, he's the one who will have to encourage the practice in them. He can give examples, guidelines, and — importantly — clear authority to carry out the initiative. He can coach them on how to analyze and present ideas. He should be nearby to lend support so that their ventures have a good chance of success.

COMMUNICATION

When we were children in school, teachers only lectured. There was very little response from us because we were shy. We were not willing to ask questions because we were taught that when elder people speak, you're not supposed to make any comments. If a student asks a lot of questions the teacher will think that he is naughty or is trying to show off.

– Thai manager, Japanese manufacturer

THE PROBLEMS OF ASSERTIVENESS

Westerners like to hash it out, get to the nitty-gritty of a topic or a problem, even if it means raising voices or occasionally banging the table a little. Some take great pride in their beliefs and opinions, and will fight for them, occasionally at some risk to the pride and feelings of others. Opposite from the Thais —and Asians in general— Australians, Americans and many Western Europeans are taught, from childhood, to stand up and speak out, even to question the teacher.

But the hierarchichal society does not permit the risk of attack on another's pride, especially if the person is higher up on the social ladder. And even if the other is not higher in rank, his feelings have to be protected as well; Thais are quite sensitive to the "tone" of a verbal message. Words interpreted as being direct or too strong may affect whether the speaker of those words can remain effectively within the other's Cautious Circle .

The Thai tendency to refrain from giving offense results in a subtle linguistic dance that the uninitiated might easily fail to recognize. For example, in the following case, some Thais wanted to let their boss know that they thought another employee was mistreating his subordinate:

> I had an employee come to me, and I couldn't quite understand why he came to see me, or what it was he was trying to get me onto. He told a little story, being a little evasive here and there, so if I followed the stepping stones that he set, I would, at the end of the stepping stones, find something that another employee did. This is the way the conversation went:
>
> "So-and-so moved to a new apartment. Have you heard about her lately?"
> "Yeah she's been pretty sick lately. How is she now?"
> "She's still not well."
> "Oh really. Is anything wrong?"
> "Nothing serious. . .but you know. . . ."
> "Uh, no, I don't know. Is there something I should know?"
>
> And through that process, I find out what that person was really getting at. And in some instances, I remember on two or three occasions, where I've actually had the physical sensation that I'm looking behind that person, thinking to myself, "There's this person back there who wants to say something. What is it?" The key is, you have to be sensitive to this subtle form of communication.
>
> — American manager, airlines firm

However, most successful Expat managers will tell you that gaining the trust of your people is the biggest step toward encouraging more assertive behavior. If they know that you are open to all ideas and opinions, and they risk very little in asserting what they feel might be the silliest ideas in the world, then you may very well end up with a very talkative staff in the long run. Perhaps an overload of information! Thais will talk, but preferably not at the risk of offending or being offended.

GETTING FEEDBACK FROM SUBORDINATES

In a recent large-scale study of communication within an oil company in Thailand, it was found that people felt that the lack of feed-

back was a major weakness affecting communication within the organization. In particular, Thai subordinates were found to be frequently failing to report necessary information in a timely and usable fashion.

In another company, a Swedish manager had come to Bangkok from his previous posting in Stockholm. The interviewer asked him, "What is the difference between the operation you are managing here, and the branch you were managing back in Stockholm?" He reflected at some length, then replied quite deliberately, "Well, here I get the feeling that we have no problems."

After being probed further by the interviewer, he continued, "Actually, we have lots of problems here! I just never *hear* about them, that's all. In Sweden every level of staff comes to me with problems; even union workers. But actually, the Swedish operation was going along much better than this one."

The heart of the story, which is of course the big headache for the foreign manager, is the frustrating gap he feels between reality and the information which he gets about that reality.

The cause of weak feedback is, not surprisingly, a combination of at least three factors: difficulty with English; uncertainty about what is necessary to report; and the constraint we know as *kreng jai*. This constraint, among whose several definitions are "deference" and "reluctance to disturb," is frequently responsible for poor-quality feedback.

Obviously a manager needs the very best upward feedback he or she can get, and that includes especially the prompt reporting of bad news. He should spend time with his staff on the subject of feedback. If he is able to show the Thais during this process that he recognizes and appreciates their *kreng jai* (which is to some extent a show of respect for him, as well as a bit of fear), he will have helped to reduce that barrier. In time, these efforts will tend to improve feedback to quite acceptable standards, and the manager will find himself more approachable.

As explained earlier, the Thai boss of the past did not usually expect to be informed by subordinates of events going on within the organization. Why? Because he would become aware of such problems himself, through his high level of observation and wisdom, rather than need to be told about them by some junior. Accordingly, today, when it's time for his assistant, Sawai, to get a merit salary increase, the boss should already be aware of the fact; it would be unthinkable for Sawai to approach the boss about it. Indeed, if the situation went on too long, without the boss being aware of it, Sawai might even resign. And very likely he would not give his boss the real reason for resigning.

ASSERTIVENESS IN MEETINGS

Most people don't look forward much to meetings, whatever country they come from. Often enough, they turn out to be a waste of time. When people of more than one nationality are involved, the obstacles and potential frustrations are multiplied.

The following is a case of how cross cultural meetings can inhibit the participation of Thai meeting members, and lead to faulty conclusions.

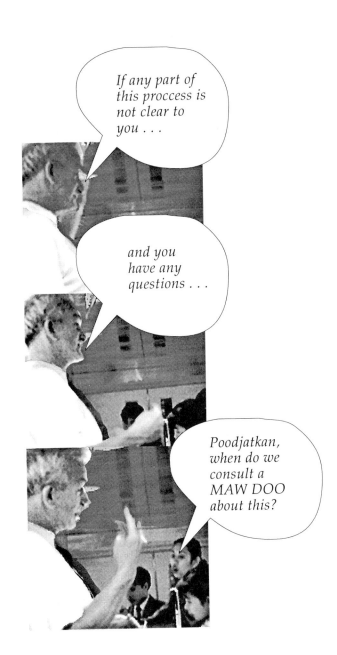

A European held a meeting in which he brought together twelve senior people, a mix of both Asians and Europeans. He hoped for (1) the best possible ideas, and (2) full participation by all the members. As the meeting progressed, ideas were thrown about quickly and frankly. Westerners did more of the talking than the Asians, at times interrupting each other in their enthusiasm. One of the Thai members listened carefully but said nothing. Later in the hall, the European asked the Thai his opinion of the meeting. As they talked it turned out that the Thai had a number of different ideas from those brought out in the meeting itself.

In this case, the roots of the problem lie with both the Thai and the Expat.

The Thai probably faces a number of obstacles in a meeting like this. The heaviest of all is probably the use of English — his second language. In most Thai schools, the teaching of English stresses reading and writing rather than speaking; these are the skills they test at examinations.

When it comes to the special skills of "meeting-English," much more is required than just spoken fluency. The Thai needs to be able to exchange ideas in a rapid give-and-take fashion. He has to be able to ask for clarification of others' ideas, question people, perhaps contradict them. If he wants to give a few of his own ideas, he has to know how to present, defend, and pursue them, among people who may not be receptive. Such skills require high ability to handle confrontation, in addition to using language of a fairly sophisticated level.

And as related earlier in this section, a second obstacle for the Thai may be the cultural background which comes with his education. Few schools encourage children to speak up voluntarily. Few Thai teachers have the habit of asking for volunteers for comments or new ideas. But more important, a person's peers often don't look favorably on someone who speaks out; someone who wants to look good — a show-off. Many Thais feel that it 's one's peers who most inhibit an individual from expressing himself at meetings — as much as any chairperson. The greater the size of the group and the rank differences among the members, the greater the difficulties of speaking up.

Finally, many Thais are not used to the ground rules of western-style problem-solving meetings. In standard brainstorming, for example, members are urged to offer even partial or "wild" ideas in hopes of encouraging a novel or inspired solution. But in the Thai concept of meetings, like the school system, rewards are given for *correct answers*, not hunches. One gets sanctioned for being incorrect. Said one senior Thai executive, "In school we get rewarded not for taking initiative, but for getting the right answer."

As for the Expat chairman of the meeting, he had a hand in creating some obstacles for the members. In spite of encouraging everyone to contribute, he allowed the native English speakers to dominate. By permitting interruptions, he created a certain pressure to contribute quickly, thereby requiring even greater fluency and skill of "debate" which further disadvantaged the non-native speakers. The Expat probably didn't allow members much time to think or prepare their positions in a systematic or orderly way. Finally, the group itself was probably too large and diverse for members to feel relaxed and frank.

In the West, the concept of participation in meetings or work groups is a democratic element particularly important for problem-solving exercises. Each member who attends has usually been invited because he has some special interest or expertise which can contribute to the outcome of the project. As the meeting goes along, if a topic comes up which touches one member's specialty, he 's expected to express himself, voluntarily. He doesn't need to wait to be asked. And even on other topics, if he wants to clarify a point or probe another member's line of reasoning, he has the right to do so, albeit with a bit more tact and good manners. If such a member were not to contribute to an area about which he was knowledgeable, the members would think him indifferent or irresponsible — in fact, not accountable.

What Thais have traditionally expected of meeting members has been absolutely different. For many, the word "meeting" implies a very large group arranged in rows, convened to receive information or policy from the chairman. As members, their duty was to listen, not to exchange views.

The person who chairs cross-cultural meetings has a reasonable chance of achieving participation, as well as results, with a few guidelines in mind:

1. Select members carefully, for relevance to the topic. Keep the numbers small, and try to minimize rank differences.

2. Provide a clearly written agenda in advance, and specify your expectations of each member.

3. Check the opinions of certain members individually in advance, in order to reduce members' reluctance and demonstrate your interest in what they can contribute later in the meeting itself.

4. Give good ground rules on the use of language, and provide equal time for all. Monitor carefully the way people speak and listen to each other.

5. Try to use a rather orderly meeting style, asking members for their views, one by one. In this way, individuals can contribute without volunteering.

6. Establish a "safe" cordial *gan eng* atmosphere, where members feel welcome and comfortable.

7. Allow small-group discussions in Thai, with summaries later by representatives in English.

8. Have someone write up the results, to make sure everyone has really understood or agreed to the same things. Make sure follow-up is thorough, every time.

When Thai colleagues are asked for their views, it's important to give them a considerate hearing, so that they can express themselves "as satisfactorily as they might do in Thai." If someone's idea isn't good or workable, the rejection needs to be made with courtesy (*hai kiad*) and a show of fundamental friendly support.

A middle level Thai manager related a different experience entirely:

The senior Swiss executive asked several of us Thais for our opinions on a new marketing proposal. When my Thai colleagues made their proposals and comments, some were put down very abruptly. Expressions like "nonsense!" I felt the Swiss weren't really serious about our ideas. At that point I was very upset. But I decided: This is nevertheless a strong company; it basically has a very good system and I can learn a lot here for a few years. But when I've learned what I need, I'll move on.

GIVING INSTRUCTIONS

A Belgian lady told her driver, "Samarn, please go round at 0930 and pick up my husband, then take him over to the doctor's office. After that I need to go to the hairdresser. Pick up the children at 1500. Got it?"

Samarn said "Yes."

Little did the lady know that there are about six levels of "yes," and Samarn's yes was way down on the list. Hardly surprising that Samarn did not do everything he was assigned to do that day.

When a senior person gives an instruction to a Thai who is very junior, and the junior doesn't catch it, it is not natural that the junior will say so; nor is he likely to object if he feels the instruction itself is impractical or has faults. The force of *kreng jai* is great. When an efficient Thai supervisor is giving an instruction, he or she tries to be on the lookout for any non-verbal signs that the subordinate didn't follow it. He'll be watching, almost unconsciously, for any hesitation in answering, lack of assurance, a smile that doesn't belong, or a nervous shift in body position. He doesn't put too much stock in the "yes" by itself. If he sees any of these non-verbal clues, he will stop and go over the instruction another way, taking more time and checking for understanding at each step of the process.

When a Thai says, "Yes", he has probably made a rough English translation of the Thai word *"khrap"* or *"kha"* (literally "I ask to receive"). This Thai word, when spoken with the right degree of enthusiasm, can be correctly interpreted as a show of understanding and commitment. But when spoken without energy or conviction, it could mean as little as "I acknowledge the fact that you have said something to me"; and not a lot more.

As he continues to build better communication with his staff members, the supervisor needs to encourage them to ask questions and — more difficultly — to raise objections or reservations in case they are given an instruction that they don't think will work. "If you see me going in the wrong direction, you need to tell me, or all of us might end up with a bad result." A concerted effort to open up communications like this will, in time, bring Thais to the point where they do speak up. But it takes *much longer* than in countries where the skills are already emphasized in the family and school system.

Here are a few guidelines to reduce these obstacles and ensure more successful instructions:

1) Before assigning any task, take a moment to see if the other person is free from other work and is ready to listen. (This is surely good management anywhere, but particularly in Thailand.)

2) Give instructions in small doses. Check along the way.

3) In an office situation, use a friendly written note on occasion, to clarify or confirm details.

4) Take more time to check for understanding. But try to do it as a way of showing you are interested and supportive, rather than that you doubt the employee's abilities. This may seem a fine point, but many Thais actually decline to ask questions precisely for fear they will be seen as incompetent.

THE OBSTACLES OF ENGLISH

During a recent seminar between Thais and Expatriates, a survey was given to determine how successfully the Expats believed they had communicated their ideas to the Thais. The Expats' estimates ranged between seventy and ninety-five percent. When the Thais were surveyed, however, they reported having grasped only between forty and eighty percent. The difference between the Expats' perceptions and the Thais' perceptions, bears serious consideration. The average gap is frequently as great as *thirty percent*.

Most Thais who have not been educated overseas have learned their English from Thai teachers of English. The emphasis in their classes has been on reading and writing; little on listening, and even less on producing oral English. As a result, when English is being spoken to them, most Thais need to follow four steps:

1) translate it into Thai;
2) think of the response in Thai;
3) translate the response into English;
4) finally speak it out in English.

After a few rounds of this little procedure, the unfortunate Thai is already far behind and starting to get discouraged.

It is absolutely essential for a Non-Thai to speak in deliberate, simple, non-slang, carefully-pronounced English. It was said by George Bernard Shaw, "Half the words in the English language are not spelled the way they are pronounced, and the other half are not pronounced the way they are spelled." If this alone is not daunting enough to Thais, then the different accents of the English they hear ought to finish them off. Thais have to listen to English spoken by Swiss, French, Americans, Dutch, New Zealanders and Japanese. Many Thais working with Australians continue to be startled when asked: "How are you to-die?" It helps to be aware of one's own regional accent, watch one's slang, and slow down at least twenty percent.

When a Thai fails to understand something, some foreigners respond by speaking louder. Rather than clarify, the louder volume often tends to be heard simply as noise, but the meaning is still misunderstood. A better path: rephrase the sentence, slow down, and pronounce it more deliberately. And look for non-verbal clues that tell you the listener is still getting only half.

WRITTEN COMMUNICATION

It's a good idea on occasion to confirm an understanding by putting it in writing; this ties in with the strength which many Thais already have in English — i.e., their reading ability.

But when it comes to writing in English, Thais are often reluctant to do it. In the work situation, one reason is the fear that they will express their point poorly; then other colleagues may see their bad grammar. They also seem to view the written word as having a heavier weight, a greater permanence than it seems to carry in the West. This means the risks are greater.

On the social side, Thais rarely answer invitations in writing; still less do they write thank-you notes. These gestures are exclusively done in person.

In a case where there is conflict, it is often prudent to avoid expressing that conflict on paper, except as a last resort. It is usually better to work out the conflict face to face, and privately. One very significant reason for avoiding the written expression of conflict is that it tends to limit further opportunity for the conflicting parties to maneuver, or more important, to compromise. Thais usually try to preserve as long as possible their flexibility when trying to come to an agreeable resolution. As one Thai expert said, "In Thai companies, reports and 'positions' are rarely written because the Thai feels he cannot change it and must be committed to it." *

EVALUATION, CRITICISM AND DISCIPLINE

THE JOB PERFORMANCE REVIEW

In the West, there is the concept that criticism can be constructive as well as negative. It is seen as a potentially useful tool to improve one's skill and performance. Even in the West, of course, the system has its pitfalls and anxieties, but multinational companies engage constantly in evaluation and criticism. The "job performance review" is a prime example, a most carefully-developed model based on this concept.

Not so in Thailand. The word, "criticism" (*wijaan* in Thai) conveys at best a neutral meaning. More often, it's viewed with apprehension. And criticism is generally taken in a much more personal

---

* Chainarong, 1988

way than is the case in the West; it is not seen as a purely professional matter. As a result, it has been consistently difficult to make the job-performance review operate successfully in Thailand.

What, then, does a prudent Thai boss do when he wants to correct a fault or improve a way of doing things? His first step is to express, in a general way, his satisfaction. Then he proceeds to suggest in quite a gentle way, that "There's just one small thing that would improve the way you are already doing this." The employee usually gets the message, and appreciates the consideration implied by the boss' approach.

DISCIPLINE

Both supervisor and subordinate know that from time to time the supervisor may need to intervene to put an employee back on the right track. But in Thailand, the process needs to be done fairly, respectfully, and quite a lot more gently. Beginning at the initial orientation, it helps to be thorough. This is particularly true with hourly workers or domestic staff. Systematic and friendly follow-up helps assure that things will go as hoped.

Whether in a large organization or in the home, it is necessary to set up some controls in order to minimize "leakage," or control petty corruption. When you send servants to do your shopping, there is no substitute for knowing some of the prices yourself. Early in the game, follow up each market trip by checking carefully, and with keen interest, the prices paid. Even though your permissive Expat predecessor may have ignored loose change and allowed leakage, you yourself have the right to establish at the start any procedure which makes you comfortable. And with all such matters of control, it is easier to start off with control than to try to restore it when it has unraveled.

Among drivers, warehouse keepers, purchasing agents and other office staff, there are sometimes cases of making private arrangements with garages and suppliers to record purchases or services which have not been supplied; or at inflated prices with a rebate to the staffer. One's policy about these matters should be made clear right at the start. Early checks may be made on actual work done, and good records kept of repairs and maintenance. Spot checks of market prices will serve as reminders that you run a "tight ship." While Thais do appreciate a nice boss, they don't particularly admire the fool.

LOSING ONE'S COOL

When things go wrong, it is often difficult not to get angry. Rest assured that Thai supervisors also get angry. But what is crucial is the way anger is expressed; it determines whether the manager will achieve better discipline (and hence his goal) or simply create "noise" without understanding — or worse, resentment. According to the traditional Thai view, one of the "skills" which a person has supposedly learned as part of his rise to high rank and authority is the ability to be moderate (Thais refer to it as *sam ruam*, explained in Chapter Two) in his extreme shows of emotion. The man who "explodes" is sometimes seen as losing his own face as much as that of his subordinate. As the skillful manager tries to project mastery of his furious emotions, his flashing eyes will generally do more than enough to convey the intended message.

DISMISSAL

How dismissal is done can be rather crucial. The senior person may express regret that her own working needs and those of the subordinate don't seem to fit together. She may assign more tasks, or more difficult hours, trying to overload the subordinate and making the job more demanding than before. But she would make great effort not to undermine or threaten the dignity of the employee.

If all goes well, the boss will succeed in giving the employee "room to maneuver" whereby the individual will voluntarily resign. One Thai senior manager recounted how she was able to get an unsatisfactory subordinate to resign, "simply by ignoring him for two weeks." No dismissal was necessary.

If the boss has to take the initiative, she often tries to cushion the blow by giving plenty of notice, assisting the subordinate in finding another job, and providing a separation payment comfortably in excess of what is required by Thai labor law. But if a violation is clear and/or involves dishonesty, most Thai managers believe that the company should provide no special extra compensation. "Absolutely do not be generous," they say.

If a subordinate feels that his boss has genuinely been as fair and humane as possible, it is very unlikely that he will feel bitter or vengeful.

FOSTERING TEAMWORK AMONG DEPARTMENTS

Our company is rather chopped up. We have eight business groups. When I arrived I found they were like eight little kingdoms and they each had their own style. And they sometimes didn't like to work together. That was my number one issue. There just was no common objective, no striving for the common good. Corporate well-being was secondary.

— American managing director, manufacturing

Because hierarchical relationships and loyalties are so important within Thai organizations, the average Thai staff person is used to getting instructions from his or her boss, and is normally very re-

That's an interesting idea . . .

. . . but you are from another department . . .

sponsive to those instructions. When it comes to *lateral* requests from people in other departments, who have a different boss, responsiveness and easy cooperation are not necessarily automatic. There exists much less "leverage" between peers across departments, and less belief that cooperation is a normal part of one's duty. Thais see this lateral kind of cooperation as a favor, given voluntarily; *not* part of their duty.

This "selective" approach to cooperation is especially true when there is a "specialist" in the company who is not really part of the hierarchy, but who can be important to many departments in the organization. A British managing director explains:

> There have certainly been some spectacular failures in terms of trying to set someone up as a functional person who works across the whole company. It just absolutely fails. If you appoint someone, say, two layers beneath me as the expert or the support for a certain area, he will be accepted by his immediate peers in the department he's in. If he tries to move across to another department, then effectively he's got to go to another manager with the same status as his manager and work with him. And he finds it difficult reporting to two bosses. And if he tries to do it by saying, "Well, actually the managing director has asked me to do this," then he gets a problem because he's in conflict with his line manager.

> There's a great consciousness of the hierarchy. The people who work in a way which is not sympathetic with the hierarchy feel uncomfortable and can be seen to be pushing themselves forward. It doesn't get done unless the whole management hierarchy around it is sympathetic to them. You can't just give a junior manager a role, with the support from his senior manager, and say, "work across all departments." If the senior manager is prepared to sweep a path for the junior manager with the other senior managers, almost chaperoning him around, then it works because it is like the fellow moving with his hierarchy above him. But if the senior manager is not prepared to proactively encourage the junior manager in his role, then nothing happens. The junior manager feels he hasn't been properly empowered.

Outside of having to "move with the hierarchy above you," good cooperation and teamwork are still possible if you focus on the relationship side of doing business . If you or your subordinate have built up goodwill with people in other departments, and they like you, cooperation is likely. Or someone, or some people, may want to cultivate mutual cooperation in anticipation of a "tit-for-tat" in the future. They may also want to avoid conflict in the future by helping you out in the present.

DEALING WITH THE GOVERNMENT

SOME HISTORICAL BACKGROUND

Management of government was traditionally based on a system called *kin muang*, to govern (literally "eat") a district. An individual assigned by the King to oversee a district was all-powerful; he could collect taxes and utilize free labor. He turned in part of the proceeds and produce to the royal coffer as a kind of "royalty". Since every man was also bound to go to war when needed, the governor would sometimes form and lead a troop of soldiers to support the King.

Immediately under the King were two chief ministers — one to supervise the military, the other to look after the administration of government. In the reign of King Chulalongkorn (1868-1910), eleven "functional" ministries were created, somewhat along western lines. One of the new ministries, significantly, was Education. And King Chulalongkorn also established a school within the Grand Palace for training officials to enter the various royal departments.

Because of its historical origins, the primary loyalty and responsibility of the earliest civil servants was naturally to the King (and, later, to one's superior within the expanding system), *as distinct from being due primarily to the population at large.* Only more recently, around the turn of the century, did the notion of service to the population begin to emerge. This fact is quite different from traditions of civil service in many western countries, where the average citizen feels that the civil servant is paid by the citizens' taxes to facilitate the needs of the citizenry.

The early Thai "civil servants" naturally held very high status in society, drawn as they were from the elite rather than from the broad rank-and-file. Though they are now no longer just from the upper ranks, some of the prestige of their earlier rank remains today, and much of the power as well. Consequently, *it is frequently at the civil servant's willingness or discretion, rather than because of duty, that he may provide a certain service.* Even in modern times, when the pay of Thai civil service has hardly kept pace with salaries in the private sector, the government official retains a position of greater prestige, influence and connection than his counterparts in many other countries. For these and other reasons, when ordinary Thai citizens approach civil servants for assistance or service, they do so with a higher degree of deference, in order to create or nurture good will, and inspire a willingness to assist.

DEALING WITH "OFFICIAL" THAILAND

Given this background, there are a few guidelines which can help smooth one's dealings with "official" Thais.

The Key (once again) is Relationships: Probably the most important aspect of an effective official relationship is the effort put into creating and maintaining a framework for cordial personal relations with those officials with whom one expects to deal over the coming months. Compared with the West, it is usually much more important in Thailand to spend time getting to know one another, as a prelude to getting down to business. If the official feels comfortable, liking and trusting the foreigner as a person, a tone is set which tends to smooth the way for business dealings. In the future, if there are misunderstandings on details, the chances are better that the official will be understanding or flexible, simply, perhaps, because he or she *likes* you. The good relationship can lead to assistance with cumbersome rules and regulations.

Early sociable courtesy calls need not wait until all the technical preparations have been completed. Indeed, not having all the details worked out can further emphasize the personal nature of the early meeting.

Don't Focus On Just the Top Dog: One knowledgeable insider also suggests that the Expat should cultivate relationships with those *below* the official who occupies the highest position in a given agency, for he may not actually have the greatest power to help or thwart you. More junior officials, who carry out the agency's routine work, are crucial in the approval process, and are often just as concerned about their power and status.

The managing director of a prestigious oil company recently reported:

> I went to see the director-general about this problem we were having with transportation. I told him that the minister himself had given me his personal assurance that we could get support on this problem. After hearing my claim, the director-general said, "Well, what the minister says is one thing; what actually will happen is decided right down here."

The real work of many ministries and the interpretation of regulations are accomplished to a large extent by those below the political-appointee level; by people who have been around for years — a stable, experienced cadre of technocrats and bureaucrats. These individuals transcend political changes. For a foreigner to recognize and take time with some of these officials will create reserves of goodwill which can yield long-term benefits. These contacts should be fostered and nurtured throughout the life of the project. George Hooker, a consultant with long experience working with Thai government agencies, summed it up:

> Foreign executives who spend a few hours each month on their government relations rarely have complaints, and usually receive a sympathetic hearing when government problems do arise.

Patience: Without such efforts to create good relationships, it is common to find Thai officials rather indifferent to the needs and technical concerns of the foreign investor. They may assume that the foreigner is here because he wants to come rather than because the government invited him. Why, then, should an official jump to respond when things go wrong?

There is also the need to "orient" or educate certain officials whose understanding you may need. It may be that a Thai official, born to a non-commercial family and sometimes without actual business experience, can't instantly appreciate the full consequences of an investor's technical or financial problem. The time taken to introduce and explain will generally be well spent.

In situations requiring urgent action, a foreigner can expect to find that things don't often happen very fast. Certainly, his own priorities are not the same as those of the officials.

Decisions in government are often made collectively. Such a system may appear defensive, certainly slower than in some other countries, but it tends to protect individuals from the loss of face which would inevitably result from a decision that turned out badly. It also serves somewhat as a hedge against government officials making private arrangements to their own advantage. The existence of a group review-committee tends to insure against corruption (as in the case of a contract) or against a personal vendetta (as in the case of a minor official who is being investigated by a superior for malpractice in office).

If one's paperwork is timely and in excellent shape, and one has good personal rapport at the highest levels, a manager's delays tend to be few in comparison with others.

Finally, the foreigner should try his best to understand how the Thai bureaucracy works, accept realities as they are, and work as skillfully and cheerfully as he can within those realities.

SIX

Social Roles Outside the Office

Apart from the normal management tasks which every foreigner expects to perform, there's another aspect to "the job" that requires his attention outside the office. A Thai's private life and professional life often meld together, and an Expat manager who understands that fact can better attain his twin objectives of gaining results on the job and developing team spirit.

> You have to work hard to create a sense of family. That means that there are weddings and funerals and engagements and visits to the hospital, and unusual situations that come up, and boom, you have to take care of those things. You participate in them, whether you want to or not. You sit through the chanting of the monks for as long as it takes. Just by showing up it demonstrates your sensitivity and interest. You could probably even sit there and read a comic book the whole time! But the fact that you have come is very important. You realize that it is important to that individual. And that individual will always remember you for taking the time to respect his or her personal needs and environment. This is all part of being successful in this society
>
> — An American Old-hand in Thailand

107

SHOULD I GET INVOLVED?

The phone's been ringing off the hook. This month's sales report was due three days ago but you know you won't see it for another three days. Communication with your staff means scrambling for the few Thai words hiding in the recesses of your memory while trying to decipher their English, a mangled mess wrapped in subtlety. The home office wonders out loud about whether you have the ability to make deliveries on time. And your wife wants to fire the maid . . . again.

You have had a hard day and you just want to go home, drown in a hot bath and a couple of beers.

Unfortunately, there is a funeral service for the father of your sales manager that evening. Do you go to the service, or do you go home and forget about your troubles? It's not hard to think of an excuse. "I'm truly sorry, Manot, but I have an engagement tonight that I just cannot break." Manot, the picture of complete understanding, will nod and tell you not to worry about it. Not all Expats go to functions like these.

But let's say you decide to go. You drag yourself down to the funeral ceremony and you play the part of the solemn Big Boss with the soft heart who has come to pay honor to his manager and the spirit of his dear father. The cash contribution you bring, which will help defray the heavy costs of the funeral and cremation, and the wreath you had sent, which has the name of your company on it, are both very much appreciated. However, it is especially your presence, and the status and prestige that might be inherent in your position, that will make the greatest impact. This is *hai kiad* in very good form.

And your sales manager will probably never forget it.

You didn't have to go. But because you did, you may reap unexpected benefits: The staff may somehow seem more attentive. The monthly sales reports are miraculously on time. And what do you know, it's Manot who has introduced you to your latest maid, one whom your wife actually gets along with.

In the West, work life and private life tend to be completely separate worlds, worlds that infringe upon each other's territories only on the strict discretion of the individual. But in Asia, a region where agricultural values still carry some weight, the line between one's work world and social world is often rather thin. Thai society does not demand that all workers of the same company associate with each other outside the office. But it does tend to follow that participation in social affairs, ceremonies and customs facilitates the working relationship among members of a group. Particularly if one is senior, it can set the tone for the entire team. As you are not Thai, the Thais don't expect you to know their ways, at least not right away. But if you happen to do so, they may be more than pleasantly surprised, accepting you as a member of their extended family, and thus wanting in their hearts to extend cooperation and kindness above and beyond the call of duty.

The rest of this chapter describes some of the most common social events, both Buddhist and secular which you might encounter during your work life in Thailand.

BUDDHIST FUNCTIONS

When an Expat participates in a Buddhist religious ceremony, he or she is not viewed (at least by Thais) as being any less of a Christian, Jew or Muslim. Certainly the foreigner is not seen as disloyal or hypocritical toward his own faith. They regard the foreigner's joining in as a show of goodwill, respect, of willingness to participate in the Thai way, with no compromise of principle involved.

Here's a list of religious functions where an Expat might find opportunities (or obligations) to be involved.

OPENING CEREMONIES

When opening a new factory or office, Thais will usually recommend inviting a group of monks (usually nine, an auspicious number) to conduct a *phithi peud*, or an "opening ceremony". The senior monk will set the appointed time, perhaps something like 6:47

A.M. In such matters it cannot be said that Thais lack a sense of time; here they are punctual, practically to the minute. The foreign executive couple can expect to play a central role in presenting offerings (making merit) to the monks; their senior Thai colleagues will gladly guide them through the process. No need to fear appearing a little clumsy; Thais often do, too. But the effort is the main thing and is very worthwhile; by lending one's presence to the event, it achieves an essential sense of well-being among the entire Thai staff, and harmony with the ubiquitous spirit world.

For those of you who feel such opening ceremonies are a waste of time and money, think again. There are many Thais who feel that nothing bad will happen without a ceremony, but there are many others who feel that there is no point in inviting danger. Stories actually abound of offices haunted by bad spirits, with unexpected bits of bad luck and even buildings collapsing. And on reflection, it turns out later that proper measures were not taken. If so many people are going to worry about these eventualities, and so few are going to argue against it, why tempt fate?

Bring in the monks.

FUNERAL CEREMONIES

When someone dies, there are three distinct ceremonies that make up the full funeral procedure:

— a bathing ceremony in which the dead person is cleaned and dressed, and close friends and relatives pour water over the right hand of the deceased;

— a period of mourning which may last from a week to one-hundred days, during which family and friends can make merit for the dead by making offerings to the monks;

— and the final ceremony, the cremation of the dead.

Only close relatives and friends attend the bathing ceremony. For the prayer evenings, invitations are sent by word of mouth, and notices may appear in newspapers to attend one of the prayer evenings. The Expat would quite likely be invited to participate. Everyone, whether close or distant, will try to come to the cremation ceremony, which is frequently held a hundred days after the death.

It is quite common for an Expat executive, especially if he or she has been in Thailand for a number of years, to receive invitations to cremation ceremonies. In some cases, the invitation may come from someone whom the Expat does not actually know personally.

When attending a memorial service, it is appropriate to arrange for a flower wreath that visibly bears, in Thai or English, the name of the company or individual who made the contribution. As funeral ceremonies can be elaborate, expensive affairs, a cash contribution will always be de rigeur. The amount you give may vary, but careful consideration should be given to the rank you represent. Ask a senior Thai for advice so you do not offer less than is expected according to your position.

Occasionally, an Expat may be given the honor of making a presentation of gifts to the monks. Such "gifts" (again a form of merit-making) will have been prearranged by the sponsors themselves. Male worshipers present contributions directly to the monks, by hand. As women are not allowed to touch monks, gifts are handed over, placed on a piece of cloth or a handkerchief, in order to avoid direct contact.

Finally, in the case of loss to a very senior or close Thai colleague, the company may sponsor one of the several evenings of chanting at the temple. The manager himself will serve as one of the hosts, and take the lead in most of the procedures. Again, his senior Thai colleagues can guide him or her through the steps.

Expats may wonder, "In my large company how am I going to decide whose funeral I ought to attend?" A very practical answer was this one:

> I make it my business to know about every case of sickness (especially hospitalization) and death among staff or their close relatives. We have a system for this. If the situation involves a direct report, I make a visit myself. If it's for a lower rank, my direct reports do the same; but I will always send a card or flowers.
>
> .– Dutch manager, transportation firm

MONK ORDINATION CEREMONY

It is a custom in Thailand, particular in the rural areas, that during a man's lifetime he should spend some time in the temple as a novice or a monk. He may become a monk for a brief period ranging from a week or two to a few months, but if he finds the experience rewarding, he may extend the period indefinitely.

To enter into monkhood is to give a man spiritual experience which is considered an important part of his total educational and personal development. It is especially seen as a way for a young man to make merit for his parents.

Most organizations, government or private, make it a policy to allow a man to take leave for the purpose of the ordination. As this custom is widely followed in the rural areas and somewhat less so in the cities, business organizations which have large numbers of employees with rural backgrounds will face the occasional extended absences of certain male employees.

Ordination itself is predominantly a religious ceremony. At the same time, the celebration is as secular as any other joyous affair. Friends, relatives and social acquaintances are all invited to join in. If the event takes place in a village, the entire village helps with the work of preparation and joins the celebration. Usually parents and well-to-do relatives will help pay for religious articles and provisions needed for the ceremony, or the period of monkhood which follows the ceremony.

If an employee does express a desire to become a monk, the company may partially sponsor the ordination. Better still, the foreign manager provides a personal cash contribution, a more heart-felt act than drawing from company funds which he later claims on his expense account. The employees will recognize the difference.

THOD KRATHIN

During the month of October, there is a ceremony called *Thod Krathin*, which signifies the end of Buddhist Lent. At this time, some companies will organize a merit-making project to help a needy temple. Frequently the temple is far away in a poorer part of the country, or in a location where the company has field operations. The staff get together and plan an overnight outing for employees and their families, where donations and other offerings are made to refurbish the temple. Outdoor games are usually held among staff and local villagers. If the Expat and his family decide to go, the gesture is much admired. If they can eat Thai food along the way, so much the better.

When driving along the roads leading up the mountains or towards the beaches, you'll often encounter buses or trucks packed with smiling faces, off to *bpai tiao* – which means eating, drinking, singing and dancing with a bunch of good people. Small companies, or sections of large companies are often taking trips to all parts of Thailand. You might expect a merit-making trip during *Thod Krathin* to be a solemn affair, but it usually turns out to be *sanuk*, or "fun", a feeling that may very well carry over into the work place.

SECULAR FUNCTIONS

HOME PARTIES

An American couple in their fifties had just arrived in Thailand and wanted to get better acquainted with Thais, so they started with the husband's office colleagues. They sent out printed invitations to ten Thais and ten Americans—with the letters "R.S.V.P." in one corner.

The returns came in: Ten "yes'es" from the Expats. Three "yes'es" from the Thai.

Who showed up?

Ten Expats. No Thais.

If a senior Expat organizes an official function at home, say for a visiting dignitary, his subordinates will usually be willing to attend. But if it is a purely social evening, many Thais will not be very interested. The general view is that it is not their idea of *sanuk*. They know that they may have to use English for several hours with people they know very little. And it will be talk, talk, talk. Even table manners may be formal and confusing. And will the food be any good?

The average Thai idea of a good time is a gathering of friends and acquaintances in a favorite restaurant. Restaurants are more flexible as far as space is concerned, and they can concentrate completely on eating and talking without worrying about running out of food or cleaning up afterwards. In addition, restaurants provide the preferable option to home, which is a rather private place that a Thai usually shares only with their closest of friends. Finally, nobody has to worry about when it's polite to go home!

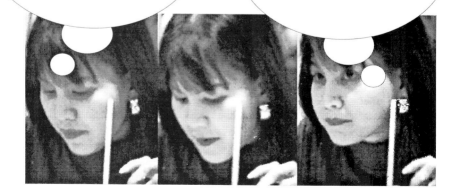

Quite often, a Thai who resides in a house will be living with extended family members whom he feels might be inconvenienced by a party. ("Where will we put all the guests' cars?" "Do my grandparents have to get dressed up and participate?" "Do we have to send grandma upstairs where there is no TV?" "If a *farang* attends, does the cook have to prepare two sets of dishes?") They may seem like minor concerns to many foreigners, but they are major concerns for the large Thai family living under a single roof, particularly if the Thai host cares greatly for the comfort of his or her guests.

If you decide to go ahead anyway . . . :
Having mentioned some of the obstacles, it is also true that many Expats have organized extremely successful events for Thai and foreign staff at home. Indeed, a few such parties have been so popular that everyone looks forward to a repeat event.

If you do plan to have a home party with members of your company, a little more thought than usual might have to go into who to invite and how many people to expect. Due to the hierarchal and relationship-orientation among any group of Thai, they will be highly sensitive to not being invited to a social function. One American manager learned that he can't even select the people he invites to his own party. According to one of his Thai managers:

> When the boss first used to give parties, he was very selective in who he wanted to come to his home. He would tell me who was coming and I would tell him, "If you invite this man, you should also invite his boss." He said that he didn't like that man and didn't want to invite him. I said, "You have to invite him." I told him that because of his position in the company, one should send such a person an invitation, and then perhaps tell him what type of party it is in a way that might discourage him from attending.

In Thailand, Westerners have also had difficulty predicting how many people will come to their party. Most of the English-speaking, overseas-educated Thais will know what "R.S.V.P." means, but may not attach the importance to it that Westerners do. The way food is served in different cultures may reveal one clue about why. Thai food is usually of the variety where several dishes are laid out for any number of people to pick and choose from. Western dinner affairs more often consist of dishes like steaks or fish fillets that are served to individuals, not a group. Thus, many *farang* will need to know how many steaks and baked potatoes they should prepare, give or take a person or two.

One manager, however, had the opposite problem where he invited his staff to his home and some people felt compelled to attend, at the expense of their own private plans. Somehow, the Thais believed the party to be one of a slightly formal nature, where attendance would be more favorably looked upon.

> One time, people were afraid to tell the boss that they couldn't attend his party, so they tried to rearrange their schedules in order to attend. When he finally heard that four people of ten had tried to change their plans to accommodate his party, he got upset and decided to cancel his party. His thinking was that it's okay just to tell him that they cannot go. Since this was causing people stress, he decided this was the best way to do it.
>
> —Thai manager, American airlines firm

To the *farang* manager, a party meant as an enjoyable evening among friends turned into a maze filled with walls built from bricks of *kreng jai.*

Guidelines:

In the event that you are keen about having a number of Thais come to your home, and have them enjoy the experience, a few guidelines may help:

1. Make sure your invitation is given *personally* to the Thai, face to face, with sincere enthusiasm that you want him or her to join.

2. Try to be sure that one or two of the Thais (especially senior or influential ones) will definitely come. This will reassure others whom you may invite that they won't be the only Thai at the party.

3. When people arrive, encourage people to mix for a while and get to know one another. But gradually allow guests to speak to whomever they want, in whatever language is comfortable.

4. Have plenty of food. Don't spend too long on cocktails as Mediterraneans do. (2230 is really a bit late to start eating. . . .)

5. Buffet style is better than a formal sit-down affair, where the table setting and cutlery can be formidable.

6. Consider some games. Card games and other low-stake "gambling" activities minimize the language differences and may lead to screams of raucous fun for all. Ask Thai colleagues for their own ideas; better still, ask them to help organize the events.

7. Due to the genuine respect and affection the Thai people have for the Royal family, avoid negative references to the Royal Family, as some Thais will take great offense at any comment or act that suggests disrespect toward the monarchy, or Buddhism for that matter. Care should also be taken to avoid references to Thailand as a third world nation as some may interpret your statement as words of arrogance.

Pictogram of a typical Farang's First Party In Thailand

Pictogram of a successful Farang's Party In Thailand

BIRTHDAYS

To celebrate the birth of a baby by presenting gifts is, perhaps surprisingly, neither traditional nor common practice among most Thai people. When it does occur, it seems to be an adaptation of the Western custom. And since such celebration tends to be viewed as a family affair rather than a social one, gifts from those outside the family are not expected. Occasionally in a small company, when a baby is born to one of the Thai staff, those who feel close to that staff member may contribute baby articles. With larger companies, senior executives are not expected to give on such occasions except, if they wish, to one's close colleague or secretary.

In general, Thais do not arrange celebrations of birthdays. Some celebrate only when an individual reaches either the auspicious ages of sixty or seventy-two, key years in the charmed twelve-year cycles of Buddhist belief. On these landmark birthdays, the focal point of the celebration is merit-making. Most people do this by giving alms and releasing captured animals. For those of a more modern bent, children and relatives may give a western-style birthday party in honor of the individual. If you are invited to such a function, you may be asked to sprinkle specially prepared water on the celebrant. Although not essential, you could bring a gift appropriate to the status of the giver and the birthday celebrant. Money, in this case, would not be appropriate.

In the case when the birthday of a member of your office or company becomes known, it is sometimes common for a small party to be held in the office. Gifts from individuals or the group will usually be presented. A cake donated by the manager (a nice example of his *nam jai*) might also be greatly appreciated. Indeed, one company feels that the "personal touch" by the boss can go a long ways towards building morale:

> To Thai people, little personal touches are very important—touches like a smile, like knowing about the family of your employees; like recognition of birthdays. I implemented a system where we send birthday cards to all the staff. We don't use the company cards—we buy every card, cute ones for about fifteen baht each. Three or four days before the birthday of the employee, we have the managing director sign the card, and then send it to their home. I

would say everybody appreciates it. Supposing a flight attendant has just received a card, and it happens that the managing director is on board. She will say, "Thank you so much," ever so happily, even though he didn't really do anything. It's the company's money, but because it's handwritten, they think, "Wow, the boss, he remembers me."

— Thai manager, American airline firm

WEDDINGS

Marriage has probably the least religious implication of all the major events in a Thai's life. At wedding receptions there are normally a large number of guests, including close family members, relatives, friends and more distant social acquaintances. Expat members of an international company are very likely to receive invitations to the wedding celebrations from their Thai colleagues, immediate subordinates, or rank-and-file staff members in the organization. Most Thai colleagues would feel honored if the Expat were actually to attend.

On the other hand, if the executive feels inundated by work and other social affairs, and chooses not to attend a wedding ceremony, by Thai custom, he or she may simply send a gift or make a contribution in the form of a money certificate. With money, it is common that other members of the staff will not want to give more than the most senior person in the organization—in order not to be seen as trying to outdo the boss. For a moderate-size company, which has between one and a handful of Expats, the contribution would normally be somewhat less for a junior person's wedding and somewhat more for someone more senior. At the same time, in order not to limit contributions by others, the Expat executive may make it known that his or her amount should not limit others in what they want to give.

If a gift is presented, as in the West, articles that may be useful for setting up a new home are given. Gifts which have sad or inauspicious implications in the Thai culture should be avoided. Examples of these include items in black color, handkerchiefs, or sharp items like serving knives. Some people feel that it is better to give articles in even numbers rather than odd, such as six glasses rather than five. The wedding gift can be arranged to be sent later or be taken along when attending the wedding. Typical Bangkok wedding receptions are held in hotels where there is a reception desk to accept wedding presents and take note of who gave what.

It is not the custom in Thailand to acknowledge gifts with written thank you notes. However, this practice, or lack thereof, does not imply that the gift is not appreciated; it is merely that Thais tend to be rather restrained in the outward expression of thanks, another example of *sam ruam*.

As a senior guest at a wedding, you won't be surprised to learn that you, the Expat, will probably be asked to make a speech. You're asked to give one more honor to the event. The idea here is to make it short and sweet.

> A very special long-term employee of mine was finally getting married. So I worked up a careful speech in Thai. I got a Thai friend to help, and wrote out the words in large phonetics.

> When the time came for my turn, in this room of over 200, I started out. I could hear some people murmuring "Wow, he is speaking Thai." Then, after not more than about thirty seconds, they all returned to their table conversations, and I still had two or three minutes of speech left."
> —Belgian manager, pharmaceuticals firm

NEW YEAR'S DAY

New Year's Day, the one that corresponds with the Western calendar, is a fairly recent "tradition" and has been celebrated increasingly in Bangkok and in provincial town centers. On this occasion parties are held, food and entertainment are offered, gifts are exchanged, and a large number of people take vacations up-country.

Aside from the normal exchange of gifts among friends, New Year's Day in cities and towns is also the occasion when people choose to express their respect, thanks or appreciation—to people in their social and business circles—by presenting a gift.

When presenting a gift to people of social prominence and influence, such as powerful military personnel, politicians, tycoons, officials and well-connected friends, relatives or social acquaintances, once again the value of the gift is determined by the roles and statuses of the giver and the recipient, as well as the nature of the relationship. A bottle or case of whiskey, or an appropriate amount of delectable hard-to-get edibles are popular. In this case, the purpose of the giving is often just to nurture the relationship, rather than to express thanks for any particular deed or service.

For the business community, it is common or even standard for companies to hold parties or organize trips as a show of appreciation to the general staff. It is also common to reward outstanding performances, particularly among sales staff or major customers, with gifts or organized trips. Customers are often given such articles as key chains, calendars and bottles of whiskey. A special customer with a large volume of purchases may get an air-conditioner, a television set or a refrigerator.

Managers of multinational organizations may take some of these local customs into account, together with long-standing company policies of their own.

Sorry about Sunday, but I make so many new friends at the golf course . . .

We love . . . to feel . . . alike . . .

SEVEN

Shifts, Jolts and Progress in the Thai Business Culture

At the hotel I was general manager ten or twelve years ago, I can remember vividly that Thais were taught to bow quite low when someone senior walked by. The *wai* still exists, but the act then was something more respectful and sincere. The junior staff today, the ones who are high school seniors and first year college students, they don't feel they have the same obligation. They feel they got here on ability. This guy's the boss, but so what? Ten years ago, if one of the senior managers walked around, they would be standing at attention and today, they couldn't care less. The European culture sort of went out the same way. And you can see those changes happening here.

— American hotel executive

123

YOUR PAST, THEIR PRESENT; YOUR PRESENT, THEIR FUTURE

Perhaps Thailand is developing normally.

Foreign residents in Thailand, who have to cope with the country's uneven progress in its infrastructure development, environmental problems, pollution and so forth, naturally wonder sometimes where the country is going.

So do the Thais.

It is easy for foreigners arriving in Thailand today to forget that their own nations and people went through a similar stage of development. For example, as an American old Thai hand relates, the USA didn't become a modern nation overnight.

> If you were to look at America in the the 1860s or 1870s, when there was a big gold rush in California and thousands of miners headed West and inundated San Francisco, the infrastructure began to creak and really couldn't handle all those people. So San Francisco went through a tremendous phase of upgrading its infrastructure: building sewer systems, transitioning from horse-drawn carts to electrical trams. And so Bangkok is basically going through a similar stage, as a consequence, in the first instance, of the Japanese having decided to make Thailand a manufacturing base.

He added that we may miss the point if we look at the inconveniences and troubles seen in Thailand as simply "problems." It makes more sense to view them as merely *lifestyles in transition*:

> Let's look at telecommunications. When I first came here, I couldn't make an overseas phone call from my home. One of the managing directors of a multinational company got so frustrated one weekend because he couldn't get through to his boss on the phone in 1984, that he just gave up and closed his office on Monday and moved to Singapore.

> Well, eventually enough telephone lines were installed and international communications improved and caught up with the times. Before we had only

telexes. Now we have faxes. I can direct dial to my children in California. So this is just one facet that has worked itself out.

Although I still can't drink the water here—as I wasn't able to drink the water back decades ago either—there is an opportunity for more Thai people to work and produce bottled water. The Electrical Generating Authority of Thailand, even with the more than five hundred industrial plants foreign firms have built in the last eight or nine years, has managed to keep up with the growth in energy consumption. You'll also find that there is an excellent long-term plan by the government that will take at least a decade, maybe longer, to curtail pollution to the point where it's not as serious as it is now. This is a normal progressive change.

The premise suggested here, then, is that the Thais are actually walking down a road not so different from those which previously industrializing countries began to travel not so long ago. Change and even progress, though halting and uneven (as it also was in Europe and North America) is actually being made.

COPIERS OR INNOVATORS?

In 1985, several senior Expat engineers gathered to discuss obstacles to their projects in Thailand. One said—in what is quite a pungent opinion—"The thing that bothers me is that all the Thais seem to be able to do is *copy.*"

A few of us reflected on this statement. Then someone piped up: "What was it they used to say about the Japanese, around 1949?" Everyone looked at each other, and things grew quieter.

Similar descriptions were made of the Taiwanese a few years later. But the late 1980s would see the Taiwanese going beyond the copying stage and initiating original technology.

It may be that along the path to industrial leadership, the first stage is to "get it right" —i.e., get the basics down properly and copy correctly what's already known—before having enough confidence to venture into the new and the untested. This transition can already be seen today in many sectors of the Thai economy, as well as in the behavior of individual Thai managers and entrepreneurs.

THE MANY FACES OF CORRUPTION

The garbage men – city employees – come around each month to collect an extra twenty baht fee from householders.

While going to work, a Thai middle manager gets caught by a traffic policeman for cutting into the bus lane. He "squeezes" two hundred baht into the policeman's hand to avoid a trip to the station.

The producer of a new film wants to sell lots of tickets, so he pays a famous critic to write a flattering review.

A company's purchasing manager gets a large and expensive gift from a supplier who hopes to secure a large chunk of business.

A senior official is able to facilitate a large international company's contract with the government in return for a significant contribution to the bank account of a close relative.

How should one interpret events like these? How do Thais interpret them?

When it comes to certain small payments for services, such as garbage collection and many others, we find most Thais taking very benevolent views toward paying a little extra. They recognize that people at the lower end of Thai society are paid pitiful wages, and it doesn't hurt to help them out. To some it's seen as a small way of making merit. The same is sometimes said for junior-level policemen who are also paid very low wages. Some at more senior levels may try to supplement their incomes by receiving payments from illegal establishments like massage parlors and gambling dens. Until policemen are paid more, it is said, they will do what they can to increase their income. Whether this is true remains to be seen.

As for payments at the "higher" end of the scale, i.e., payments to those who already have lots of money, most Thais hold very different views from those just mentioned. This is corruption and nobody approves of it. But at the same time it is difficult for them to avoid the system and play by other rules. Perhaps a comparison could be made with the health systems of certain Western countries in which the cost of health service is dreadfully high, and the average person can barely afford to insure himself against sickness. Yet the service is essential, and the system is the only one available, and it's so complex that the individual has no choice but to accept it.

Understanding corruption needs several perspectives, and we ought to look well beyond Thailand to develop a broad and realistic outlook of our own. In one neighboring country, corruption in the Customs Department had become so extreme, the government was foregoing such huge sums in tax money, that finally the entire Customs operation was contracted to a private international contractor. It was only then that customs duties began to flow through more proper channels.

Societies of some more economically developed nations have grown intolerant to naked displays of corruption, resulting in strict

127

anti-corruption laws together with more sophisticated enforcement. But as long as money and power are motivating forces for people, corruption will exist. In Western countries, corruption tends to be hidden. To make sure corruption remains disguised, large companies may hire batteries of lawyers to help them tiptoe around unpleasant obstacles of legality and taxation.

In the years ahead, foreign business interests (as well as the Thai people themselves) will demand that more teeth be added to the existing laws. Thailand will become an increasingly straightforward place to do business. Westerners may feel even more comfortable as rules are more reliable, while at the same time corruption (as in the West) takes on more sophisticated forms.

BOOMING TOWARDS THE GLOBAL INDUSTRIAL SOCIETY

Since 1986, Thailand's economy has been burgeoning. In the five-year span from 1985 to 1990, Thailand's per capita GNP, energy consumption, and (unfortunately,) the number of cars on the roads all increased by about one hundred percent. Land prices all over Thailand soared. Hotels, condominiums and office buildings burgeoned. One colleague tartly observed, "The crane is the national bird."

Much of the growth was spurred by the boom in foreign investment. Fired by a strong yen and a strong global economy, the Japanese led an investment blitz in Thailand and much of Asia that made heads spin. In the early 1980s there were only seven foreign chambers of commerce. By 1994, there were seventeen. The Japanese chamber of commerce in Thailand is Japan's biggest outside Japan, with close to 1,000 companies listed as members. Following Japan's lead in Thailand came Singapore, Taiwan, Hong Kong and Korea.

This progress can often be unkind to tradition. The once attractive canals of Bangkok have been replaced by dusty, crowded roads; skyscrapers crowd temples into the obscurity of shadows; and many of today's Thai youth prefer the air-conditioned comfort of shopping malls to home. Progress has also been unkind to some Thais working under foreign management, yet who still expect traditional management methods. The way work is done is also undergoing a dramatic change.

INVISIBLE FOREIGN CULTURE

An Expat arriving in Thailand can see immediately that he needs to learn new ways in order to deal effectively with Thais; he is literally living with Thais twenty-four hours a day. But take the average Thai middle manager, working for a multinational in Bangkok. How much direct contact does he or she have with a foreigner during an average working day. One hour? Fifteen minutes? Based on such infrequent direct contact with the Expat, it's hardly surprising that the Thai may see little need for cross-cultural skills; he is in a way, "shielded" from the need. Besides, he says, "Thailand is my country, and I get along fine."

But actually, the international company which he has joined has an "invisible company culture" all around him; it is saturated with cross-cultural factors. Consider: The company's concept of hiring on merit; the need to be frank and assertive in the case of bad news; the need to get things done by deadlines; the standards and methods expected in performance evaluation; integrity, delegation; accountability. In short, the company is loaded with elements of Non-Thai culture. All of these concepts translate into various expectations which the management holds as *standards for behavior and performance*, and they are used as criteria for promotion. We have seen over the years too many Thai employees who are not very aware of these expectations; people who have good intellects and high potential, but display a certain reserve, which comes across to outsiders as an apparent lack of self-confidence. Many were never really briefed on what foreign company culture is—its values, customs, and approaches—and why. As a result, they advance much more slowly than they could otherwise have done.

Being thrust into the fast-paced, highly competitive global market, white-collar Thailand has had to adapt to Western and Japanese management methods and concepts: computer systems, stricter accounting; return on investment; management by objective; quality control, and a host of other exacting systems. Thai workers and managers, especially those working for foreign firms, are being forced to play the game by a whole new set of rules. They are getting used to and succeeding with these new ways, but the transition isn't so easy.

129

LEARNING TO SKI – A CASE STUDY

His office is austere, and so is his manner. He asks questions directly and demands straight answers. He'll bang the table when he's upset and criticize you in front of others. He does many of the things the experts say you particularly shouldn't do when managing Thais. And yet, he's a success.

In August of 1989, Trevor Jones* became managing director of an unprofitable, one-store family supermarket business. He is a rarity in the retail business, or any business outside the hotel industry—a foreigner in charge of a Thai company. In 1994, the company celebrated the opening of its twentieth branch; its accounts are well into the black.

As Mr. Jones explained, the company was a typical family-style business. Thick with managerial levels, managers isolated themselves within the fiefdoms of their departments. According to one of the Thai managers working there, they had full authority to do as they pleased within their departments. People were hired without serious regard to cost. Employees and managers alike were known to abuse rules on attendance and work hours. Nothing was documented; no attempts were made to pass know-how downwards to subordinates.

After years of changes in management and store locations, the Thai owners of the company decided to bring in outside "professional" help. They felt a foreigner with expertise in Western management practices would be able to bring the discipline necessary for expansion.

And discipline he brought.

The first thing this managing director, an Australian, did was to introduce computers and the software necessary to begin the foundations for information control. Previously, as is typical with many family-run businesses in Thailand, there were no management systems. The methods of running the company were stored solely in

*Not his real name

130

the head of the owner or family executives. The less the business is documented, the harder it is to verify facts. But the harder it is to verify, the more haphazardly decisions can be made.

By installing computers to document all aspects of the company's business, verification of facts by a large number of managers became possible. Thus, as more managers in the company had access to more information, they were also given more responsibility to justify decisions made in their sections and departments—whether they wanted that responsibility or not.

The implementation of computer systems was the first shot in the campaign to spread responsibility for the activities of the company to a larger number of employees. For instance, before Mr. Jones took over the company, decisions on overtime or new staff hirings were made without thorough examination of facts. Now, he explained, it's different. As he described his approach:

"You have to give me answers. You can't just sit there. You can't just tell me you spent x amount of overtime. I want to know why." By doing this, the manager is more alert, he's aware, he's awake. For example, we've told all the departments, you can spend five percent on overtime. That's all. If you want more than that you have to seek approval. Apart from the month when we have *Songkran**, we have eleven months out of twelve where we never exceed five percent. And the job is still done. "Now how did you use twenty pecent before? Where did it go?"

There's waste because there's no control. You come in and say you want to hire one more staff at the office. Okay. You can have one or one hundred if you want. But go away, come back and justify it on that piece of paper. Why do you need it? What is the staff you want to hire going to do? Put on paper what you want and give it to the personnel manager.

To foreigners from industrialized nations, this procedure may sound like common sense. But to a traditional, family-run operation, it can come as a series of rude shocks. But Mr. Jones didn't stop there. Bar codes were introduced. Extensive training programs were created. An in-house distribution network was developed. A computerized ordering system was created for the branches. A

---

*Sonkran: An annual festival and holiday in April

costly security system to prevent external as well as internal theft was introduced for all stores. Change, change, change.

> If we don't do this, we can't do anything. We can't develop. There's a time that's going to come—and it's going to come real quick—when staff is too expensive and you can't get them. Every year we get a ten percent increase in the minimum wage. It may not sound much to you, but this policy that became effective in April affected 405 members of my staff. Where do you get the profit from? So we have to go to computers, more sophisticated systems, to more management control and so on and so forth.

> You can't just throw people at a problem. That's the old Thai way. "If you have a problem, put ten people there." Look at the car park. Go into a department store. There are just too many people at those places with too little to do. The time is rapidly approaching where we cannot afford that.

The Thai managers who work for Mr. Jones have grown—somewhat grudgingly—to see the logic. It is recognized that Change has worked for the betterment of the company, at least in economic terms.

But it is a reluctant acceptance, and the cultural or psychological consequences may not be evident to the participants. According to one of Mr. Jones' managers, the speed of change is discomforting.

> We were pessimistic because we were used to the old system. So when he introduced the new systems, we automatically said, "No, it cannot work. It cannot work." But finally, it worked. Before, we were spoiled, and we didn't have much work because we had only one store. We could do whatever we wanted. But now Mr. Jones wants a report for everything. Too many reports! For some people, it's too much work. But Mr. Jones still wants this and that. And they don't have enough people because of the turnover. It's difficult for you to work if staff resign. And you have to control your overtime too. With less staff, how can you control the overtime?

But they *are* controlling the overtime. They *are* doing the reports. They are getting the job done. But they can't relax and enjoy what they've accomplished because there is always something new to learn. *Gan eng* is a wistful memory. Like inexperienced skiers flying down the slope, gasping at every bump, they have to concentrate and keep their eyes out front at all times, doing their best to maintain their form and keep up with their more experienced leader.

Their muscles are taut as they fight to keep the edges of their skis in control of the ice, while their leader is is nimbly zipping ahead, apparently strong in his belief that practice makes perfect.

Jones knows this course very well. He's been in this business in Asia for twenty years and he feels he knows how to maintain the balance between pushing the best out of his people without breaking them. He has made all aspects of the company's management transparent, set rules and regulations in manuals that no one, not even the managing director, is exempt from following; and he takes the time to answer any question or explain any decision with the force of logic and experience. He believes that he can teach his people to ski expertly down this course. And so far, his ideas and methods have been rewarded with success. Thus, his people have begun to believe in the systems.

> Trust is the word. If they can understand the systems and the controls or what the business is like, and they can see that what we are aiming to achieve is right, then you're halfway to making it work. Because they accept it. And they trust you. And when you do it once and it works, and then twenty times and it works, something in there is right.

Mr. Jones pushes his people hard and they accept it, but only because he pushes *himself* as hard, and their efforts have been rewarded with accomplishment. However, any wavering on Mr. Jones' part, any major inconsistency in his management policy that occurs may, by his own admission, cause a backlash of resistance by his people that could significantly slow down the pace of development. The Thais generally prefer a more relaxed, enjoyable place of employment and the word on the street is that Mr. Jones' company is neither of those things. There's no question that some of the enjoyment—and indeed pleasure—has gone out of the job. And consequently it is not an accident that keeping down the turnover rate—partly a result of the constant pressure—is one of Jones' biggest challenges.

You, as an Expat manager, will probably be bringing your systematic work style to the Thai work place. The challenge will be to implement your management policy or work style, and struggle to maintain control and consistency, or expect half-hearted efforts by a Thai staff who have yet to believe in the systems you bring. You may find Thais less used to going all out to reach goals and achieve objectives than you are, because they may not see what's in it for them or the local company. If they are not very used to justifying decisions, it may be because they never really had to do so before. They may be less used to looking long-term because the competition was never really tough enough to make it necessary to do so. In addition, you may not feel there is time to develop relationships; there's just too much pressure, and it may not be your style anyway.

Add to this the fact that in most multinationals, every two to three years a new Expat comes in with a new system different from his predecessor's. And the Thais know that when the Expat leaves, it is they who will have to live with the system, whether it suits the local environment perfectly or not.

It is in crucibles such as this supermarket company where Thais are learning to accept and utilize new technology and consistent management systems to their advantage. Coupled with the 800,000 Thais* who go overseas to work and study annually, a new generation of Thais are learning how to ski with the best.

SOME VIEWS FROM WITHIN THE REGION

It is commonly believed that the Japanese in Thailand are having a far easier time in getting along with their Thai employees than Westerners. To some extent the Japanese have been willing to fit within the existing framework of business mixed with politics, treating their people well in order to retain their long-term services and encouraging dependency linked with dependability. This, however, doesn't mean they don't have trouble; they do. Japanese standards can sometimes be too exacting and rigidly demanding for the Thais. And on occasion, the Japanese can be rather brusque by Thai standards. Explained a Thai manager working for a Japanese company,

> What I have found is that the Japanese are very highly intelligent. They are sometimes perfectionists. And they expect everybody to be as intelligent and

---

*Thailand in Figures 1992–1993

134

as perfect as they are. So when (a Japanese) communicates with people, he has a hard time. Sometimes he cannot talk to anybody, even his secretary. He gets mad all the time, moody. Some Japanese think that if they put on the pressure, it works. But sometimes, for the Thai, if there is a lot of pressure, they cannot think. They're scared. They get paralyzed.

Although Japan can be said to retain many elements of village-oriented culture, the values of its businessmen are much more re-sult-oriented than the Thai businessmen they work with; thus some of the problems.

Similar differences are reported by Thais who work with Singaporean and Hong Kong business colleagues:

> When our Hong Kong manager comes into the office in the morning, he usually gets right down to business. "Is the report done?" "What are the production figures?" He doesn't take any time to ask about us or make small friendly conversation.
>
> —Thai manager, Hong Kong-Thai joint venture

When the Thai thought about his frustration over this, he realized that he expected the Hong Kong people—as fellow Asians—to understand the Thai much better than they apparently did. If they were Europeans, he would have had no such expectations; he wouldn't have been so surprised or annoyed.

The more Thailand develops economically, the more the Thais, too, may be accused by others of being impatient "perfectionists." As the Thai manager working for the Japanese firm reflected, he is beginning to find it a lot easier than before to empathize with the Japanese:

> We export some vehicles to Laos, so we went over there to look at the outlets. Now we understand the Japanese. Before, the Japanese criticized us, the Thai, for being lazy, and not having a systematic way of administration. Of course, we don't feel good about those criticisms because we feel we are doing our best. But when we went to Laos, we criticized the Lao people for the same things. The Japanese, they have experienced a lot of things, so they can see what the Thais are lacking. But when we go to Laos, we get mad at the Lao because we can also see what is lacking. There are differences in development between these three nations.

And among the rest of us as well.

You know, I'm still a bit confused about these Thai values . . .

Well, why not take a look at these books on your right?

SELECTED BIBLIOGRAPHY

Adul, Wichiencharoen, *Social Values in Thailand*, Bangkok, Social Science Review No. 1/1 (1976), pp. 122-170.

Alpha Research Co., Ltd., *Pocket Thailand in Figures 1994*, (Bangkok, 1994)

Anuman, Rajadhon, *Essays on Thai Folklore*, (Bangkok, Fine Arts Department).

Ayer, Frederic L., *Managing With Thais*, Text from a speech given at Thailand Management Association, *The Voice of the Nation* (July 28, 1976).

Boonchu Rojanasatien, *Some Fundamental Changes Needed to Get Thailand Moving*, Speech (June 29, 1979).

Buchanan, Sherry, *Firms Count Cost of Failing to Study Expatriate Stress* International Herald Tribune (June 26, 1985).

Burns, Wayne, *The Business of Bridging Cultures* (Bangkok Post, March 13, 1986)

Casse, Pierre, *Training for the Cross-Cultural Mind* (Washington D.C.: Society for Intercultural Education, Training and Research, 1980).

Coates, Austin, *Myself a Mandarin*, Memories of a Special Magistrate (HongKong: Heinemann Asia, 1983).

Cole, Michael, John Gay, Joseph A. Glick, and Donald W. Sharp, *The Cultural Context of Learning and Thinking* (Basic Books, 1971).

Cooper, Robert and Nanthapa, *Culture Shock: Thailand* (Singapore: Times Books International, 1982).

Chainarong Indharameesup, *The Relevance of Western Management Training: The Thai Experience*, Paper presented at Montreal (McGill University, November 1988).

Condon, John, *With Respect to the Japanese* (Intercultural Press).

Cooper, Jilly, *Class* (London: Corgi Books, 1981).

Creffield, David, *Face: A Tradition Under Fire in the Business World* (Modern Asia, March, 1984).

Evers, Hans-Dieter (Ed.), *Loosely-Structured Social Systems: Thailand in Comparative Perspective* (New Haven: Yale University Southeast Asia Studies, 1969).

Fieg, John, *A Common Core: Thais and Americans*, Revised by Elizabeth Mortlock (Intercultural Press, 1990, with further revisions)

Galants, Steven P, *U.S. Firms Learn to Bridge Cultural Gaps* (Asian Wall Street Journal. July 20-21, 1984).

Gurevich, Robert, *Khru: A Study of Teachers in a Thai Village* (Pittsburgh: University of Pittsburgh, 1972. Ph.D. Dissertation, University of Pittsburgh (unpublished) (1972).

Hofstede, Geert, *Dutch Culture's Consequences on Health, Law and Economy* (The Hague: Institute for Training in Intercultural Management, 1987).

_____ *Motivation, Leadership and Organization: Do American Theories Apply Abroad?* (Organizational Dynamics, Summer 1980).

_____ *Culture's Consequences* (Beverly Hills, Sage Publications, 1984).

_____ *Cultures and Organizations* (London, McGraw-Hill Book Company Europe, 1991)

Hirakawa, Sukehiro, *Difficulties in Cross-Cultural Communication* (The Wheel Extended/a Toyota Quarterly Review, Winter 1974).

Hall, Edward T., *The Silent Language* (Greenwich, Connecticut (USA): Fawcett. 1959), *The Hidden Dimension* (Garden City, New York: Anchor Books. 1979), *Learning the Arabs' Silent Language* (Psychology Today, August 1979).

Hall, Edward T. and William F. Whyte, *Intercultural Communication: A Guide to Men of Action*, (Human Organisation, Volume 19, No. 1, 1960).

Hollinger, Carol, *Mai Pen Rai* (Bangkok: Asia Books, 1977).

Hanks, Lucien M., Jr., *The Corporation and the Entourage: A Comparison of Thai and American Social Organization* (Catalyst, State University of Buffalo, N.Y. 1966)

Holmes, Henry: *Headaches and Remedies for Cross-Cultural Managers* (Address given to the Thai-Finnish Trade Association, Bangkok, 1991).

_____ *School Beyond the Village: A Study of Education and Society in Northeastern Thailand* (Amherst: University of Massachusetts, 1973) (unpublished doctoral dissertation).

Holmes, Henry and Suchada Tangtongtavy, *Management Transfer, A Report for Metal Box Thailand Co., Ltd.* (Bangkok: Cross-Cultural Management in Thailand, 1982).

Hooker, George, *Contact with Official Thailand* Paper given to newly-arrived foreign Managers (Bangkok 1985, unpublished).

Juree Vichit-Vadakan, *All Change for Thai Values*, Paper presented at a seminar, *Societies on the Move: Changing Values* (Cholburi, Thailand, 1990. Reprinted in The Nation, June 21, 1990).

Klausner, William: *Conflict or Communication* (Bangkok: Business Information and Research Co., Ltd. 1980).

_____ *Reflections on Thai Culture: Collected Writings* (Bangkok, The Siam Society, 1993).

Kluckholn, Florence and F.L. Strodtbeck, *Variations in Value Orien-*

tations (Evanston, Illinois: Row, Peterson, 1961).

M.R. Kukrit Pramoj, *Education and Culture in Education in Thailand* (Bangkok: Department of Elementary and Adult Educatin, Ministry of Education, 1970).

Lanier, Alison R., *Living in America* (Chicago: Intercultural Press, 1981).

Montagu-Pollock, Matthew, *"All the Right Connections: Chinese Management Has Amazing Advantages over 'Modern' Methods"*, Asian Business, January 1991

Muscat, Robert J., *Family Enterprise in Thailand* (Bangkok, January 1987, unpublished Manuscript).

McClelland, David, *The Achieving Society* (Princeton: Van Nostrand Co. 1961).

Mukerjee, Dilip, *When Taking The Money Becomes a Way of Life* (Bangkok Post, April 18, 1984).

Mulder, Niels, *Everyday Life in Thailand: An Interpretation* (Bangkok: Editions Duang Kamol, 1979).

Nakata, Thinapan, *Corruption in the Thai Bureaucracy. Who Gets What, How and Why in its Public Expenditures* (Thai Journal of Development Administration , 18/1: 102- 107, 1976).

Office of the Prime Minister, Kingdom of Thailand, *Thailand into the 80's* (Bangkok: Business Information and Research Co., Ltd. 1979 and revisions).

Ordonez, Regina, *Employee Loyalty, Not Ability, Prized in Asia* (Asian Wall Street Journal, April 2, 1981).

Phillips, Herbert, *Thai Peasant Personality* (University of California Press, 1966).

Phillips-Martinsson, Jean, *Swedes as Others See Them* (Lund, Sweden: Utbildningshuset Studenlitteratur, 1981).

Pisit Traisuth, *My Culture As I See It: Raising a Daughter in Today's Thailand*, with Roger Welty (Honolulu, The East West Center, 1975).

Redding, Gordon, *Face and Other Inscrutables* (Asian Business, July, 1979).

Redding, Gordon, and Terry Casey, *Managerial Beliefs Among Asian Managers*, Proceedings of Academy of Management, 36th Annual Conference, Kansas City, 1976, pp. 351-355

Renwick, *If Australians are Arrogant, Are Americans Boring? If Americans are Boring, Are Australians Arrogant?* (The Bridge, Summer, 1980).

Riggs, Fred W., Thailand: *The Modernizaiton of a Bureaucratic Policy* (East-West Center Press, 1966).

Smith, Tasman, *Cross-Cultural Management Effectiveness: Interaction Process Analysis of Thai and Wester Managers Playing The Tower Contract-Management Game* (Bangkok: Oxford University Press East Asia, 1982).

Srinawk, Khamsing, *"A Nation of Caged-In Children: A Thai Tours the U.S."* (Pacific Magazine, 1968).

_____ *The Politician and Other Thai Stories* (Kuala Lumpur: Oxford University Press, 1973).

Stewart, Edward C., *American Cultural Patterns: A Cross-Cultural Perspective* (Chicago, Intercultural Network, 1972 and revisions).

Suntaree Komin, *Psychology of the Thai People: Values and Behavioral Patterns* (Bangkok: Research Institute of Development Administration, 1990)

Suchada Tangtongtavy and Henry Holmes, *Communication, Teamwork and Training: A Report of an in-depth Study for Thai Shell Exploration and Production Company* (Bangkok:Cross-Cultural Management in Thailand, 1985).

Suchada, Tangtontavy, *Some Differences Between Thai and Western Social Structure* (Bangkok: Wijai Wattanatham Part. Ltd. 1983).

Surang S., *The Language of the Heart* (Bangok Post, 1985).

Thompson, Allan, *Australian Companies in Thailand: Establishment and Operating Experience Preliminary Report* (Bangkok: Australian Chamber of Commerce, 1981).

Van Roy, Edward, *On the Theory of Curruption* (Economic Development and Cultural Change Vol.19, No. 1, October 1970).

Vilas Manivat and Steve van Beek, *Kukrit Pramoj: His Wit and Wisdom* (Bangkok: Editions Duang Kamol, 1983).

Vithal, *The Role of an American Peace Corps Volunteer* (Speech Delivered to Volunteers in Andhra Pradesh State, India: United States Peace Corps, March 14, 1967).

Wekman, Sidney, *Bringing Up Children Overseas: A Guide for Families* (New York: Basic Books, 1977).

Waisfusz, Bob, *Guidelines for German Experts to Increase their Effectiveness in Thailand* (The Hague: International Development Advisory Services, 1989).

Wyatt, David K., *Thailand: A Short History* (Bangkok: Silkworm Books, 1982)

Index

THAI WORDS

ENGLISH WORDS

THE SKILLS OF CROSS-CULTURAL
MANAGEMENT IN THAILAND
A SEMINAR IN ENGLISH AND THAI

How well do Thais and Expatriates in your organization communicate? Is feedback, especially about problems, good enough?

In just two days you can learn how to build a productive cross-cultural team with increased assertiveness, accountability and understanding of both the Thai and Expat ways of getting the job done.

This course offers what is probably your best opportunity to tackle the whole range of cross-cultural problems. In *The Skills of Cross-cultural Management in Thailand*, you will learn and practice approaches to problem-solving that will pay off into the future and transform a frustrating assignment into a rich and productive one.

With an alumni list of over 8,000 executives and their spouses from Thailand and 60 other countries, this two-day workshop is one of the most successful and popular in Asia.

Information about these and other team-building programs may be obtained from

Cross-Cultural Management Ltd.
25th Floor, Grand Amarin Tower
1550 New Petchburi Rd, Makasan
Rajthewi, Bangkok 10110
Tel. (66)(2) 652-9025
Fax: (66)(2) 652-9029
E-mail: crosscul@loxinfo.co.th